RABBIT STOMPIN'
& Other Homegrown Safari Tactics

RABBIT STOMPIN'
& Other Homegrown Safari Tactics

DARYL GAY

Hillsboro Press
PROVIDENCE PUBLISHING CORPORATION
FRANKLIN, TENNESSEE

Printed in the United States of America

07   06   05   04   03   1   2   3   4   5

Library of Congress Catalog Card Number: 2002115380

ISBN: 1-57736-295-0

Cover and text illustrations by Philip Neugebauer
Cover design by Gary Bozeman

HILLSBORO PRESS
an imprint of
Providence Publishing Corporation
238 Seaboard Lane • Franklin, Tennessee 37067
www.providencepubcorp.com
800-321-5692

To Daddy,
who struck the spark but never got to see the flame.
and
To Cheryl and the Fellas,
who make all the heat worthwhile.

INDOCTRINATION

Please do not concern yourself should you not know a whole lot about such technologically unadvanced goings-on as rabbit stompin'. Trust me, that's quite understandable.

Most folks hereabouts use all kinds of hunting and fishing techniques that have never made it into those slick how-to books or videos, and if the truth be told, we're still trying to get a handle on some of them ourselves. For instance, everybody who has ever floomphed down in front of a television set knows about those fabled African big-game safari tactics. But we're a whole lot more secretive about our homegrown strategies. Take my word for it: there's a heap more difference between Africa and Middle Georgia than geographical placement.

The Dark Continent has received a lot of good press for its jungles and savannas, which feature all those exotic creatures to challenge hunters. But this little corner of the world we call home hasn't really publicized its natural treasury of outdoor sports facilities. Just for starters, we have dove fields occasionally occupied by over-sized and over-aggressive bulls . . . deer woods containing some not-so-dear creatures like chiggers and red wasps . . . duck-wading lakes equipped with lurking, hidden stumps and precipitous drop-offs . . . quail country embroidered with barbed-wire fences and bamboo vines (the civilian and natural versions of concertina wire) . . . rabbit-hiding, hide-mauling briar patches . . . and swamps concealing all manner of irascible critters from gators to feral hogs to bears to C-5-sized mosquitos.

Rabbit stompin' and the other homegrown safari tactics I'm about to share with you were custom-designed exclusively for use in the wilds of Georgia. But with only a tad of imagination—yours—they can be adapted to just about any patch of real estate you're able to gain hunting access to. These brilliantly-planned(?) schemes don't remotely resemble some of the more widely-known varieties of hunting methods, but you have my personal guarantee that they have been thoroughly field-tested by me and a passel of relatives and hand-picked friends.

To make your learning experience a tad more interesting, as well as to allow proper recovery time between dreams and nightmares, the lessons have been recorded in story form. You might find some of these parables a mite hard to believe right off, but don't be overly quick to brand them fabrications. It has been said before: "I cannot tell a lie." For your edification and entertainment, however, I can stretch the truth plumb across the Okefenokee Swamp and back.

TAKING THOSE FIRST STEPS

I t all started, best I recollect, better'n twenty-five years ago, on a bitter cold morning when me and my Uncle Glynn shot each other pretty near to pieces with a matched pair of Daisy BB guns.

While that may seem a dangerous and rather inauspicious beginning to a lifetime love affair with the outdoors, I look back on it fondly now that the stinging has stopped and the welts disappeared, the latter covering a period of approximately a dozen years.

Although we were at the time allegedly quail hunting, the frenzied object of our animated actions was not a partridge, or "pottidge" as it is called hereabouts. Nope; we were doing our dead-level best to snuff out one of that ever-squawking species of winged wonder known as the blue jay—likely the prime culprit in repeated raids on my grandma's prized fig tree.

This particularly vocal and agile bird was getting more than his money's worth of use out of every limb in a six-foot pine tree. And Glynn and I were getting more than our share of round pellets in the lower portions of our anatomies. The jay's

1

tree was growing from the very bottom of a small ditch. Glynn and I were perched on the slightly-elevated sides of that depression, cocking and shooting like Midwest townfolk fighting off a Dalton Gang raid . . . and standing directly in each other's line of fire. This provided a great deal of amusement for our audience, which consisted of a vast assortment of uncles, brothers, and fathers from my mother's side of the family.

And while we're on the subject of kinfolk, let me attempt to explain right off how this conglomeration came about.

Okay. Brace yourself.

Shortly after granddaddy married grandma, his brother took it upon himself to wed her sister and then his sister got hitched up with her brother. Got all that? Neither, after all these years, has my wife, but she's getting there. Anyhow, the end result of those three marriages was a gaggle of extremely close-knit offspring, including Yours Truly. Although I was the first grandchild of the bunch, I was only five years younger than my mother's youngest brother, Glynn. Since it was five more years before the next grandyoung'un came along, Glynn and I were brought up much more like brothers than uncle and nephew. Even though the generation lines tended to blur, our family ties were and still are tighter than an old-maid aunt's corset.

But let us hie back to the hunt.

Most of our onlookers were spellbound, as if we were putting on some kind of comedy routine. They had determined right off that our whistling projectiles were targeting an area from roughly our bellybuttons on down. These were toughened old country boys every one, and seeing no danger of our putting out an eye or doing other significant damage to each other, a couple were even rolling on the icy ground in uncontrollable laughter. In my eyes, these would have been impressive displays of merriment under any other circumstances. At the time, however, I was totally occupied with drawing a bead on a blue jay and listening to Glynn squeal.

We never figured out whether insanity, hysterics, or being winged by a BB kept that crazed squawker in that tree. It was for sure that it wasn't going to take wing, although it was putting on one magnificent hopping act. It is also certainly possible that the fits of maniacal laughter the jay was suffering from kept it corraled. Meanwhile, it was for gosh-awful sure that Unc and me were being winged . . . or armed . . . or legged . . . or whatever the proper term for catching lead projectiles happens to be. Finally, it was a fact of life that there was no way either of us would have ever given up without taking that bird's scalp!

Eventually, soft-hearted Uncle Math McCrackin, out of mercy for all three of us, waved Glynn and me back out of the way, sauntered to the tree, and shooed the cackling jay off into the wild blue yonder, evidently not much the worse for wear but at least dropping a few feathers as he left. With the shooting finished, Unc and I turned our energies into tossing down our weapons and fighting each other barehanded. Ice and pre-puberty invectives filled the air as we battled for those feathers, each a trophy to be encased in a pair of spanking-new hunting vests.

We were then "asked" to sit and listen to a dead-serious lecture on what to and what not to shoot at for the rest of our days. The jay, although a pest if ever there was one, was never to be harmed again, as it was not a game bird and not meant for the table. As far as shooting each other, well, that was relegated back to the slingshot and chinaberry days we had, on this very afternoon, graduated from.

And although it would be a few years before I would actually bust a real honest-to-goodness pottidge, I was hooked on the hunting life at that point. That said, I would caution any of you who do not believe in the so-called blood sports to put this book down right now . . . or take the dire chance of expanding your education or adjusting your attitude. Let me also warn you that these sports are indeed bloody, although not necessarily as gory and heartless as the process by which your morning bacon, noon-time filet-of-whatever, or evening steak is rendered.

Let's understand one another before we go on. I am, first and foremost, a hunter. I believe in my sport at its highest level and purest form, and I make no apologies for partaking in this, one of the greatest loves of my life. I shoot with a camera as well as a gun, and capture trophies in words and on film as well as in the fur. The camaraderie of fellow outdoorsmen, the challenge of the fair chase, an unabashed admiration for the wonders of nature, and the joy of swappin' tales as well as the sharing of some fantastic cuisine have all blended into my abiding love of the outdoors.

Hope you can relate.

2

FROM ROOFING TO WRITING

D ads work in mysterious ways to shape our lives. Although mine died at the ripe old age of fifty-eight thanks to a smoking-related habit, my major regret is that he had to grow up so fast and leave us so early.

Speaking of that habit, I guess it was natural for Theo Gay, hereafter referred to as Daddy, to act like a grown man even at age nine. His own father had just died, and since there were no food stamps and welfare payments at the time, circumstances forced him to go to work. It's probably just as well that the government didn't step in with a handout; he'd never have accepted it anyway.

His jobs included plowing long, hot hours behind a neighbor's mule in an effort to support his mother and two younger sisters. He was carrying a man's load, so perhaps he felt entitled to enjoy the manly vice of using tobacco.

Hard work was Daddy's lot in life. He climbed from a child-hood as a field hand to an adult life of typically working fifteen-hour days in construction. With only a third-grade education, he developed skills that astound me even now, such as the ability to draw up house plans from simply listening to how a couple wanted their place set up. To this day I can't tell when a set of house plans is right-side up. Those who knew him believed that Daddy could build anything, including a pretty good pair of kids. I looked up to him just south of worship and never faulted him for much of anything because he always did his best by my brother and me. It was Daddy who, perhaps inadvertently, started me along the path to becoming a writer.

My life took a critical turn when I acquired my first of several shotguns from him. (More on that later.) When I had finished terrorizing teachers each school day—no, not with the shotgun—I lit out for the woods and fields to do the same to any game bird or animal which happened to be legal for the taking at the time. Daddy, making sure that my education was furthered even after those one-hundred-minute school hours had ended, rather heavy-handedly discouraged any law-breaking, careless use of a firearm, or the misuse of any animal I hunted. To put it bluntly, his ham-sized hands made some rather heavy landings on my backside on the few occasions when his lessons were forgotten or ignored.

For example, I was not to shoot anything not meant for the table. To that end, in four decades of hunting, I have killed a grand total of one 'possum—and that out of infinite stupidity.

In a hail of lead spouted along with my Uncle Austin—next-oldest brother to Glynn—five squirrels and this 'possum were popped as they exited adjacent nests on an oak limb. It so happened that I, in the excitement of the moment, terminated the largest member of the bunch, and if the truth be told, never want to see another one as long as I live. You can probably come up with the greasy reason for my attitude. Yep. I had to dress out, bake, and consume part, although it was a very small part, of that wretched marsupial. My innards still cringe at the memory. Ironically, on the weekend of my birthday each year, a small nearby town has what is known as the Possum Hollow Festival. Cooks there actually serve up cauldrons of yellowish, stringy, (yeccchhhh) possum stew as the featured course for thousands of browsers of arts and crafts. More than thirty years later, I still do not partake; won't be partaking thirty years from now, either. That, however, is getting way ahead of the story.

My days of glorious hunting and painful education were commonly referred to as the Black Death by my teachers. Finally and somewhat miraculously, I found myself with diploma in hand and enrolling at a nearby junior college. And that was a master plan for disaster if ever there was one. Not having been born with the proverbial silver spoon in my gaping maw, I went to work every afternoon after class to pay my way through this local institution of higher learning. This required setting up all my classes in the morning hours.

The establishment which provided my weekly stipend had made a finger-pointing, no-exceptions requirement: these-here hours for this-here pay. I had met that requirement right up until it came time to meet the teachers and "counselors," a term I use very loosely. Unfortunately, my counselor was a certain dean who obviously did not suffer from my infantile problem of no-precious-metal-in-mouth disease. He informed me that I had to give up an A.M. course to take at least one in the P.M. No arguments, no reasoning, no choice; it was his decision and, by gum, he had the power to enforce it! All algebraic equations aside, that equalled giving up my job, which equalled giving up my formal education. That dean has long since retired . . . hopefully to a life of forever scrubbing the black holes of outhouses . . . but I shall never forget his contributions.

My dad the carpenter quickly solved all my monetary problems, however. He provided all manner of interesting work, such as digging ditches and foundations for buildings, lugging buckets of tar and bundles of shingles and rolls of roofing paper up long ladders, and—my all-time, numero uno favorite—installing those old yellow rolls of fiberglass insulation in kiln-like upper portions of houses commonly referred to as "attics."

When the sweat ran out, the itching set in . . .

Kicking back one brass-bright "insulated" morning on one of our two-a-day, fifteen-minute breaks, I finally did it. With my tongue running in and out like a hasslin' hound's, I informed Daddy that this particular line of work just wasn't going to satisfy my life's ambition. Building things was what he had always known and was superb at doing. The talent had not, however, rubbed off on me. I abhorred it then and even now can't construct decent squares with kids' blocks.

"Well," he queried, "what do you think you'd like to do?"

"If I could make a living hunting and fishing, that wouldn't be too bad," I replied, only half-joking.

"Then do it," was his reponse.

So . . . I did.

Starting out with a mid-sized newspaper as a wire editor, I eventually weasled my way into covering sports. Since hunting and fishing are two of the great loves of my life, I offered to write an outdoors column along the way. You will discover that most employers will allow you to contribute anything extra you'd care to, just as long as no further coinage on their part is involved. Mine fit that pattern perfectly. Advanced student that I am, since that time I have acquired a Ph.D. in Applied Dove Missing from the School of Hard Knocks and Tough Shots. Also, if you've ever tried to raise a family on a writer's paltry income, you will understand that I had all the financial wherewithal of a New Delhi street urchin. The choices boiled down to becoming adept at foraging and cooking or learning to starve, since we couldn't exactly afford to go to Antoine's for filet mignon or even to the local fast-food emporium for grease bombs very often.

Deer, wild hogs, and smaller game came in remarkably handy when we were trying to live on gruel for weeks at a time. You may even be able to appreciate some of the recipes I developed during that period. They are joint products of my admittedly simple mind and desperate circumstances, but most folks do come back for seconds. We'll get to them in a bit.

But for now, as the little girl wrote in her biology report, "I don't want to tell you more than you really want to know." So let's just drop my background and evolution as a writer of sorts and get on with the parables of surviving in the wilds of Middle Georgia.

3

LESSONS FROM THE OLD MASTER

"K EFFELARE." One word; one syllable. It was a command that no professor of proper English could ever hope to recognize. But the sage old liver pointer understood it, and she knew just what to do: stop as still as death and wait for the big man to speak in a slightly softer voice. Her left hind leg quivered, as did the tip of her rigid tail, as he almost whispered: "Careful there, Belle."

But in my mind, the utterance will forever remain "KEFFELARE." It is an enduring symbol of one of the greatest men I ever knew. To me he was a very big man, and he fit the bill in both size and reputation. He was a good one, hard but fair, tough as nails, yet tender as love itself. His name was Henry Grady Hooks, he was known as H. G., and he was my grandfather.

H. G. died quite a few years back, only ten months before my dad's death, although both seem like yesterday. On the other hand, it's as if an awfully long time has passed since I could sit down and rationally think out what he meant to my life, much less write about it. One of his sons, my Uncle Kermit—older brother to Glynn and Austin—was killed in a car crash some years ago. Engraved on Kermit's marble slab is a Remington 1100 shotgun, forever pointed toward a covey of brown birds winging it for sanctuary. Maybe that'll tell you a little about the legacy H. G. left behind. That morning, and the hunt with old Belle, remain a grand part of that legacy.

With the softening of his voice, she eased ahead over the frost-hardened ground, one delicately-padded paw at a time, and into the briars. The pointer moved as if walking on nitro-filled eggshells, nose high and reaching. Every muscle was locked onto the birds, and from there directly connected to a central computer that was a mammoth man cradling an ancient, battle-scarred twelve-gauge Remington Model 11-48 shotgun. She took one last whiff, and the centuries-bred instinct told her a split-second before he did: "WHOA."

Adrenalin burning, the big man stomped through broom sage and the ever-present briars, motioning me in from the other side, and we swept past her. As the fifteen or so quail busted skyward in an explosion of feathers and whirring wings, the 11-48 spat a staccato threesome. My heretofore puny Winchester sixteen-gauge ripped off a single report and, wonder of wonders, the brown bird fell! I couldn't believe it! I had actually killed a "pottidge," as the big man called it. But the proof was in the jubilant old pointer's tender mouth: four birds had been returned, and the worn Remington held only three shells. One of those pottidges had to be mine!

There wasn't much to his praise; not the spoken type anyhow. "Pretty good shootin', Least'un," was all he ever said. (As far as H. G. was concerned, he had four sons, not three and a grandson—namely me. I was the youngest, or "least" in age, hence the nickname.) The blue eyes, on the other hand, spoke volumes as he handed over my first quail, a dishrag-limp golden nugget.

In that hallowed moment, my only tangible reward was the bird faithfully retrieved by Belle, simply one of hundreds she

had fetched for the big man. But Granddaddy's praise transformed me from a callow boy into a hunter.

And, from there, into a fisherman . . .

After the hunting seasons had ended for the year and my
heart was smack dab in the midst of shattering as it always did
when we had to hang up the guns, the big man took me "trout"
fishing.

Years later I came to know the particular piscatorial
species in question as a largemouth bass. But today's bass
fishing does not remotely resemble the trout fishing we did.
They are, in fact, distant galaxies apart, and never the twain
shall meet.

Oh sure, I'd been fishing before, and those hand-sized
bream we caught were great, even if my hand was small. But
trout were considered the greatest things motivating in water
in my little piece of the world. Take your pick, but we'll have a
world-class argument about it to this day.

There was a modicum of ceremony to trout fishing, unlike
the days we went after panfish. The bream required only a
double ration of do-your-duty wigglers from the roofing-tin-
covered worm bed at the corner of the yard. But when we went
trout fishing, Granddaddy's battered metal tackle box would
be front-and-centered and put through an inspection that
would have made Patton proud. All the while, I would be
crowding over every plug and hanging on every word of the
fish story that went with it. Funny, but the big man didn't do all
that on the brief occasions when he went by himself.

One thing you could count on when the two of us went
after those trout was that a certain lure was going to show its
face. It was called, in the big man's words, a Frog Popper, and
that's good enough for me. The first place I ever eyeballed it
was on a tiny stretch of water called Salt Lake, which looked
much more like a creek bend than a lake. Don't even bother to
ask directions; we hiked in for what seemed like years.

It was a part of the ceremony, I suppose, that when he first
threw the old plug out, something almost instantly attempted

to pop the frog out of it. But it wasn't all that easy to draw a strike, in retrospect, since the Frog Popper had no action of its own. When flung upon calm waters, it simply lay like the pieces of wood and steel it was. From there, the massive figure in overhauls . . . not overalls, if you please . . . would move approximately two muscles in his corded left forearm, and the Frog Popper would dance. Oh my, how it would dance.

The movement would be imparted through an arm-length, metal fishing rod equipped with the blue light special, reel-of-the-day of his choice. ("Spend too much money on 'em and it goes to their heads," he'd say.) The reel contained just enough black line, which mightily resembled parachute cord, to cast clear across the county.

I could hardly wait for him to teach me how to work that Frog Popper. Since then, I've read and met quite a few of the famous hunting and fishing teachers of our day; they're good, but honestly, I've never seen anyone who could teach like the big man. He could take the end of a log and make it a university of trout fishing. There would be fish down there that knew they had better sense than to bite, but simply couldn't resist; when it danced for them, that crippled old Frog Popper was just too choice a morsel. H. G.'s grizzled face would stare across the water, the bright eyes pinpointing exactly where Ol' Bigjaws was holed up: "That point there, that's where we need to start." Think I argued?

And oh yeah, I learned. I learned a lot, good and bad, as the years went by.

I watched and practiced until I could work a Frog Popper with the best of them. Then, as his own failed, it was my eyes that would have to pick out the starting points. As the years flew by, the big man would sit near me in a dove field, offering advice now and then, sometimes breaking into a distant smile I couldn't understand. Occasionally, I'd hear the deep, snarly "Chuff, chuff," laugh I knew so well and loved so much. He didn't really laugh at me when we hunted or fished; he simply sat back, enjoyed the occasion, and failed to keep the pride inside.

As I learned how to shoot properly and well, the big man was losing a little on the covey rise. He would growl, "This old gun needs a new barrel; this 'un's too short . . . too long . . . too wide . . . too narrow . . . plumb burnt up . . ."

Belle and the other pointers and setters were long gone, but they had left lessons with their aging eyes that only good dogs can teach: "He's getting older, boy. Watch out for him."

For the next few years, we went shooting whenever he had the time and inclination. The doves still felt the wrath of the magnificent 11-48. The old (by now) Winchester did a little better those days, and he would rumble with the familiar laugh when a bird fell to my gun. Sitting daydreaming in a dove field, hearing him be proud of me, it would have been a chore not to think of the heart-stopping "whoosh" the trout made when they pounced on the Frog Popper . . . or of the dogs pointing and fetching . . . or of the pottidges. . . . And it made my day to see him down an infrequent bird so that we could be proud together.

Over my fireplace these days rest two mounted trout. The one on the bottom put up the greatest battle of any I have ever caught. It is by far not the largest, only the one I will most remember. Many times since the dawn of a June morning when I caught it, I have wished I had set it free, for if ever a fish was deserving of freedom this one was. But now there rests in its open mouth a plug that has accounted for many hundreds of largemouths equally as large. Don't ask what its proper name is; the scarred wood and sharpened steel are probably eighty years old. I know it only as a Frog Popper.

But if Granddaddy was here, he wouldn't be satisfied with the size of that fish. "See that point over there?" he'd query, anticipation bubbling in his voice.

But he's not here, at least not in body, although he'll be a part of me every day until my personal dust-to-dust scenario is acted out. And I at least have the soul-soothing knowledge that when the big man was old and lagged a step or two behind, I took the time to wait on him. That we fished and hunted at his pace in those days, because in the early years he had gone at mine. In his teachings, he put up with many a mistake and misstep from me, and I only tried to repay his patience with a little of my own. I'm thankful now that I appreciated him while there was still time.

Forgive the dampness on the closing pages of this chapter, if you will. Guess I got in a hurry and spilled something when I thought I heard him say, "Well, there's a spot over there that just has to have some trout of considerable size on it. Let's take this old Frog Popper and go see . . ."

4

Renegade Shotguns

One of the most devious, black-hearted game birds of all time is the mourning dove, alias "bird of peace." Do not under any circumstances, for even a New York minute, ever allow yourself to get sentimental about this scoundrel.

In the South, opening day of dove season kicks off months of delight for hunters and shooters. Visions of doves swimming in milk gravy with a large chunk of hoecake biscuit on the side are dancing in my head even as we speak.

But opening day, not to mention the remainder of the season where things tend to get even worse, can also provide the basis for decades of high blood pressure and nightmares. Just a season or two ago, the following quaint episode involving the mourning dove threw me into something of a jam—as well as several other places.

As mudholes go, it looked rather innocent. I have seen worse, and would rate this one only about an 8.5 on a scale of 1 to 10, with 10 being the Everglades. The adolescent swamp was nestled in the middle of a winding field road, directly between the old pickup truck the two of us were in and the dove field that was our destination.

The truck's proprietor and chauffeur was a gentleman of the finest kind, Mr. Walter Foy. He was the retired principal of the local high school, and a man known and respected far and wide. I was riding shotgun, so to speak, innocent as an infant blessed by Mother Theresa. I had not realized that without having the obvious charms and thrills of riding herd on scads of brats since he had hung up his paddle, Foy's life had been somewhat lacking in the excitement phase.

He, however, had immediate plans to rectify that situation . . . as in jumping the mudhole truck and all . . . but failed to inform me of them, no doubt wanting to spring a pleasant surprise. One instant we were sailing nicely along, and the next we were simply sailing . . . then dropping off the edge of the world.

Ever notice those little round buttons on the tops of hunting caps? They are ostensibly put there to hold strips of the cap's fabric together, but it has become my belief since this episode that there is a much more sinister reason for their existence. At any rate, there is an exact imprint of one of those buttons in the top of Ol' Foy's Custom Cab. Its dimensions correspond perfectly with those of a depression in the middle of my brainbox.

I had a lovely view of the imprint up top from my position under the dash. This, of course, was after I had rocketed back downward. Somewhere during the imprinting process, my knees rapped out a quick soliloquoy on the underside of the forged-steel glove box while half a case of shotgun shells performed the Charleston along the left side of my rib cage. (Alas, while my various and sundry joints would survive quite handily, arthroscopic surgery was required for the truck's heater.)

Meanwhile, back at the flood . . .

Said flood was thanks to incoming tide from the Mudhole and was flowing briskly over the truck's windshield wipers. It had drowned the motor out, and I was going down for the third

time when the rescue team . . . in the form of Foy's hand . . .
arrived to extricate and slap me back to reality.

I soon found out why he had decided to save me.

Each of us glared at the other, wondering who would make
the initial move to backstroke out and dry things off so we
could fire the truck up again and carry on.

Foy said coyly, "Well, don't look at me. I don't even know
how to open the hood."

He had, however, learned how to keep the truck's original
manual in the injured glove compartment, so that idiots like
me could perform miracles of restarting engines. After an hour
or so of his step-by-step instructions, punctuated by echoes of
hundreds of shots resounding from the nearby field, I got it
unwet and running at last. Foy's threats of birdshot in the
backside as he slid shells into the twenty-gauge had nothing
whatsoever to do with the success of the process . . . or my
willingness to play the role of mechanic rather than hunter.

I'm still not quite sure whether Foy's sweet-shooting little
twenty-gauge fit the bill of renegade shotgun. But it's for sure
that it belonged to the same union as that renegade Ford pickup.

BUT ALL THIS HAPPENED AFTER I HAD BECOME A GROWN MAN. AND
looking back on my childhood hunts, it looks like I would have
known better. An opening-day dove shoot like the one with Walt
Foy always puts me in mind of the first few times I sauntered
out into the world with the intention of ending the promising
careers of several of those upstart young birds. I remember
them especially clearly while sitting bolt-upright in bed in the
wee hours of the morning after another nightmare about those
jaunts with my boyhood friend, Jerry.

You've just gotta get to know Jerry. He was, and remains, a
real piece of work, the kind of guy no sane pedestrian would
ever want to meet on a darkened street corner. Or a brilliantly
lit one, for that matter.

Never laying any claim to sanity, however, Jerry and I were
a regular hand-slapping, tag-team tandem of terror. Local

townfolk had even bequeathed us a catchy nickname: the Village Idiots. We were the envy of all our non-monickered friends until around age thirty, when the lot of us discovered the true meaning of the term.

Jerry was nothing more or less than your basic, run-of-the-mill moron. About the only thing he had going for him was that he owned a shotgun . . . which in those days upped a moron's standing in the world indubitably. The fact that the gun had a stock resembling a jigsaw puzzle with a couple of pieces missing . . . a split forearm bound together with that favorite repair mechanism of morons everywhere, chicken wire . . . and a rust-pitted barrel roughly as long as the Alaska Pipeline did nothing to dimish its luster in my bugged-out eyes the first time ever I saw it.

As far as I was concerned, that weapon was a top-of-the-line, gold-engraved, Belgian-made Browning, and worth at least a million marbles.

"Man alive, I'd kiss my sister for a gun like that," I fawned to Jerry one afternoon, spawning what turned out to be a black-letter day in my brief existence on the planet.

"You ain't got no sister," he growled back. Then, with a grin like a starving wolf, he remembered, "But I have. How's about kissin' her?"

"Uh, er, what about your dog instead? Or the old jackass out back that's on his last legs? He deserves at least one smooch before he turns up his muleshoes, don't he?"

Despite my pleas and protestations, the depth of his deviltry knew no bounds. Jerry at last threw into the deal the one proposition that he knew would close it: "Kiss my sister and we'll go down to the corn field and you can shoot doves with my gun."

Mister, when I was nine years old, I'd'a kissed Attilla the Hun's sister—and slapped his ugly mug to get to her—for a chance at a real live-and-in-color dove shoot. Unfortunately, Jerry's sister was about as thrilled at the idea as I was. But as soon as I had run that ugly little heathen down and finished

chaining her to a tree, I planted a smack that peeled her lips back like a 'possum gnawing persimmons. Shortly after, when I had finished running my own lips through the local car wash, I was ready for the shootin' to begin. No sir, I'll never forget the first time Jerry allowed me to touch off that excuse for a cannon.

Nor will I ever forgive him for it . . .

WHEN THE FIRST DOVE OF THE AFTERNOON CAME DROPPING LAZILY BY, I aimed carefully and gingerly squeezed the trigger. From a distance . . . the recoil knocked me just inches short of a first down . . . came a roar akin to that of a Concorde taking off. At the time I heard it, I was rolling rapidly along the ground, the movement aided by the fact that my shoulders were now in the shape of a hula hoop. The bony blades therein were beating out a drum solo of "The Star Spangled Banner," but I was in no position to either stand at attention, march, or give much of a hoot.

Strangely enough, the bird began to fall, according to Jerry, who was at least able to see it now that the mushroom cloud had disappeared. Although that cloud looked to be almost identical to the one over Hiroshima in '45, the dove seemed to have sustained no such damage as did the city. Truth be told, we never did figure out whether it had been hit or had a stroke brought on by a severe case of laugh-itis. Whatever, the bird put on one of those special aerial maneuvers that only doves have mastered, spreading its wings wide and coasting to a landing somewhere among a nearby copse of trees.

Well, "copse of trees" is a rather neat little phrase, but actually the area more closely resembled the mountainous areas of New Guinea. Didn't make no difference to me nohow, because I was determined to find that chief ingredient in grandma's recipe for dove gravy and grits. So, packing two weeks' ration of RC Colas and Moon Pies, we set off. Eventually, we were so far back in the jungle that twice we had run across Abdominal Snowman tracks when we came to a rusty old fence, a single strand of barbed wire stretched lethally on top. Luckily—or so we thought—there was a fallen log laying across the prickly stuff that could be easily traversed by two young studs in the prime of what almost turned out be severely shortened lives. So, upon it to continue the trek we hopped.

Ever heard of a red wasp?

Most folks down South call 'em "wawsts." On other occasions, such as this one, they are referred to by a host of very different terms, some extremely technical and others anatomically impossible. These wasps build nests ranging from golf-ball-sized cottages to monstrosities that cover the hidden lower surfaces of entire logs. Guess which size we happened upon.

As I clambered onto the log, an initial whirring of wings touched off a low-voltage leap, sort of like brushing against a raw spot in a plugged-in drop cord. Both of us instantly recognized the source of the sound, which did absolutely nothing constructive for our collective blood pressures. From whirring, things progressed to flapping then to roaring, sort of like an old P-51 Mustang preparing for takeoff.

And take off is pretty much what Jerry and I did, even leaving the ground like a P-51 occasionally. The roar—from the wawsts, not us—increased dramatically as they gained ground on our revved-up rears. We would hunch low and try to pull away from 'em flat-out, only to ricochet off pines, hickories, each other, and such. Then we'd bounce up, literally, and haul off in a new direction, welts rising rapidly and arms flapping like squids gone squirrelly.

Eventually, we again found our progress blocked by the fence. But this time, things were different. We cleared the barbed wire with ease, happily without ripping out any assorted extremities and becoming sopranos for life. The wawsts fell back in near-exhaustion and at last gave up and went on to bug somebody else.

Now, you may be wondering what a fence was doing in a place like this, anyways; we, on the other hand, hadn't really had a chance to sit and give it much thought.

But as we were trying to get back to some vestige of civilization, still no bird in hand, Jerry and I happened upon a rather large and somewhat displeased longhorn cow, male of the species. Jerry noticed him first, and hollered a warning from his position at the time, which was about a mile ahead of me thanks to the headstart he got. As the bull came over to chastise, exercise, and exorcise me from his domain, however, I took to my now-dragging heels and quickly made up the lost ground. Talk about broken-field running . . .

It has been my belief since that day that bulls strategically lay out their personal brand of minefield to aid and abet the chaser and hinder the chasee. When a ton or so of wild hamburger is pounding along inches behind your flappin', smokin' hightops, you pay very close attention to such things.

On the other hand, when they get their danders up, bulls don't seem quite as attuned to the layout; therefore, sudden slippage often trips up and confuses a bevy of bovines and allows said chasee to hunker down and pick up valuable real estate. Such knowledge comes only with years of pasture-crossing experience, but remember that these feats were performed by experts and should in no wise be attempted at home.

Jerry and I came back to the fence with no time to spare, a dump truck load of snarling sirloin hot on our heels. This time we simply levitated to safety—except, that is, for the bull. He slipped on something or other, went into a major-league slide, then was flung back from the barbed wire looking like a model for a butcher's cut chart. As the wire twanged like a Jimi Hendrix guitar string, all he could do was slobber, bleed, and try to stare us into oblivion.

I had landed in a heap, out of breath and fully convinced that death was at hand if forced to take another step within the next twenty-four hours. But just then a sudden rustle a foot from my feet caused my parked brain to lurch into overdrive and screech, "SNAKE."

Adrenaline is pretty amazing stuff, you know? And not just for bulls!

Seconds later, I waved with the breeze from the top of an eighty-foot pine, gazing downward. I could see that the offending rustler was not a snake after all, but the initial object of my chase: that stupid dove. He was rolling on the ground, cackling noises emanating from his pointed beak, totally unable to fly.

That, heh-heh, was to prove his ultimate undoing.

As I came down the tree, fortunately limb by limb and with no sudden takeoffs except for the last ten feet, the bird tried to get away again. But my final, spleen-splitting pounce was rewarded, and snatching him up, I ended all his worldly problems with a case of assault and battery that would have made prime time's top ten shows of the year.

Later, as we triumphantly tripped back into the field at last, another dove flew over. Jerry shoved the gun at me, urgently whispering, "Shoot, shoot." After that came the fastest trip home he ever made.

I'd'a caught him, too, if only the tread on my hightops had held up!

5

MORE SCATTERGUNS I'VE KNOWN

Believe it or not, and my wife refuses to, there was a time when I did not possess a shotgun of my own. If you stop to think about it . . . and I did quite often as a piddling lad . . . borrowed shotguns are much like bucking horses. Once one throws you, the best thing to do is grab aholt of it again and jump right back on. However, the gun my friend Jerry owned (the twelve-gauge Atomic Special discussed previously) is credited with creating a radical change in my views on that subject. But, you see, Jerry had *two* guns.

Although our fathers were the best of friends, they naturally didn't agree on all subjects pertaining to such hirsute activities as hunting and fishing. To my knowledge, and no one would know better, Daddy owned only one shotgun in his lifetime. You will read more about it later, for it is a subject which I love to discuss.

But Jerry's pa hauled in scatterguns in case lots, and some of them found their way permanently into his moron son's four hands and that curved hook on his fifth arm. Jerry's backup to the Atomic Special, also affectionately known as Ol' Clavicle Crusher, was a .410 bore single-shot. This was an innocent-enough-appearing piece of hardware that probably wouldn't give a gnat shoulder problems recoil-wise.

When the bandages that resulted from my first dove episode and the resulting knockout by the twelve-gauge had been removed, I again got the itch to go hunting. After all, what I had been through was enough to make anybody want to kill something. And that .410 was mighty interesting to my still-tender shoulder.

I had saved up a little money from my movie part . . . the starring role in *The Hunchback of Notre Dame* . . . which I landed without even having to wear makeup thanks to that blasted gun blast. But on opening day of dove season, I still didn't have quite enough for the automatic I lusted in my heart after. So, Jerry offered me the loan of the .410. After putting him through my own version of the Spanish Inquisition, I accepted.

My, but that was a sweet-shootin' little jewel, too, the first time I pulled the trigger. Of course, the dove that was the object of this misbegotten affair flew on with its heart blown through its ears, a special talent that only doves, quail, and ducks seem to possess. But at least I was conscious enough to realize it this time around.

No matter, because here came a big drove of fifteen to twenty more birds, homing in to light on my cap. Chuckling with mad scientist glee, I quickly popped the barrel open, grabbed a shell, and rammed it home.

Almost.

I should have known it was too good to be true. The cussed single shot's ejector turned out to be as worthless as a promise from Castro, and the empty hull was lodged in the barrel like a swollen cork. There I was in the middle of a corn field jam-packed with doves, guns banging all around, and mine wouldn't shoot. Digging out my trusty Barlow knife, my first thought was to carve the stock into toothpicks fit for a troop of fleas. But I decided instead to attempt to unhang the hull and get off another shot. Dig, dig, dig . . . fiddle, fiddle, fiddle . . . rant, rave, AHA . . .

Awright, next victim. We're loaded and ready to go. Thaaat's right stupid, fly on over this way . . . just a little more . . . and BLAM. Out comes the Barlow, here fly the doves, and the beat goes on.

You'll find this incredible, and may not even believe a smidgeon of it, but along about the middle of that afternoon, I silently resolved that my dove-shooting-at career, as brief as it was, had come to an end. No more would I suffer the humiliation and hernias which went with the decadent lifestyle of a so-called lover of dove hunting. It was, sniff sniff, sadly, sniff sniff, but yea verily, sniff sniff, all over.

For a whole week.

That's how long it took for Daddy to start drawing all the pizen out. He began the next Saturday morning as he always did during dove season, by reaching up over the front door frame and lovingly hoisting down the Winchester Model 12 pump. He was wearing his frayed, tan-colored canvas vest and carrying a box of shells in each hand, so I knew where he was headed. I must admit that the knowledge didn't do much for my frame of mind, but I was firm in my commitment to a life-time of abstinence.

"Ready to go?" he queried.

"No sir, don't think I care anything about it any more, to tell you the truth," I replied. (By the way, that second word of the brief speech was always best included unless I had a sudden hankering to gum my grits for the rest of my days.)

With my reply, both boxes of shells clattered to the floor and he rushed to my side, obviously expecting me to swoon at any second. Eventually discerning that I wasn't dying or drunk ("drugs" weren't in our vocabulary back then), he dug out all the reasons for my refusal.

"Come on and let's try it one more time before you give up completely," he urged.

I finally complied.

You know, thinking back on it as I have so many times over the years, I honestly believe it never crossed the short span of my mind that Saturday morning that it was the day before my birthday. I mean, it's not like these days, when the only thing our kids expect is a new Lamborghini each year. Our celebrations were simple: if we got anything at all other than unholey socks and drawers, it was a red-letter day.

Anyhow, when we pulled up in front of the hardware store, Daddy made some excuse or other about going in for shells or whatnot. I dragged after him, still not exactly thrilled about the prospects of another afternoon fighting off heat prostration and diabolical firearms.

The white-haired old gent who ran that store was as kind-hearted a soul as I can remember. He always had a word and a grin for me, despite the fact that I constantly drooled over his hunting equipment and couldn't afford a .22 Short cartridge if he had broken a box and sold them one at a time.

"How you doin' Least'un?" he drawled as I shuffled in, calling me by my pet name. "You look kinda down in the dumps about something; never seen you this way headed out to a dove shoot."

It got started briefly, but my muttered excuse died in mid-stride as Daddy suddenly appeared from behind another counter. He was wiping down absolutely the shiniest, most beautifulest, exquisitest, brand-newest automatic shotgun ever seen in all creation. And he handed it to me.

I just looked at him, and at the old man, as they watched me. None of us said a word. Somehow, my eyes must have gotten across the message that I wanted to hoist the gun to my shoulder.

"Go ahead," the store manager said softly in his special way. "After all, it's yours."

Mine?

Unless you've been there, you will never know the love and adoration that a dumbfounded youngster felt as he locked eyes with the man who had brought him into the world and

along the early years of struggling through it. Daddy looked like he had an extra Adam's apple in this throat, and I thought I saw more than the usual watering behind his dark-rimmed glasses. For the life of me, even after shouldering and pulling that beauty down in awe for the tenth time, I still could not get a word out.

In fact . . . just remembering . . . I ain't saying a whole heck of a lot right now.

6

THE SOLID-GOLD 12, AMONG OTHERS

As you may have figured out by now, shotguns are one of my favorite subjects. My creditors also are pretty fond of them, mainly because scatterguns have kept me in hock up to my hams for years now. But there's one that I didn't pay for, at least in terms of coin of the realm. It's Daddy's Model 12 that you read about earlier. There have been several occasions when folks heard about it in a different manner. On a couple that I fondly recall, they didn't listen.

THERE WERE TWO BIG TWENTY-PENNY NAILS DRIVEN INTO THE TOP OF THE frame of our front door when I was a yonker, and in my mind's eye I can see them right now. There was nothing especially outstanding about the nails themselves, except for the fact that upon them rested my dad's prize possession: that old pump gun. He bought it the first week of September 1954, and I hatched three weeks later. For years, until I was old enough and considered competent enough to accompany him on hunting trips, I was forced to watch and bide my time on the

Saturday mornings when he would pull it down and go to the dove field, or turn out our old setter for a day of quail hunting. My longing heart always followed him out the door.

Eventually, the day came when I could tag along, although there was no way I was going to be totin' a gun. No sir, buddy; back in my early days, one served an apprenticeship to learn the whys and wherefores of proper gun safety. Young'uns today who think they have had a tough time with hunter safety courses should be thankful they never had to take the program personally conducted by Theo Gay. You did it right, by gum, or you didn't do it at all.

Upon major mistake number one, he would take away your gun . . . the worst punishment ever devised by mortal man . . . and put your behind through the Bessemer process for good measure. Now that I have three sons of my own, I see that there really should be no other way of handling the situation.

I remember with Technicolor clarity the first time I ever shot that gun. The temperature was simmering a mite over one hundred degrees in the corn field and the birds had better sense than to be flying. Several hunters had set up their stools, as did we, in chosen spots, then promptly adjourned to the shade of some nearby pecan trees. As is their wont when hunters convene, talk turned to guns. Pretty soon, two of the bigger talkers took to arguing over whose would kill a bird the farthest away. The disagreement eventually came to involve a double-handful of paper likenesses of Andrew Jackson.

I was acting bird dog for the day, remember, and was the only member of the group not packin' iron. Because of that, I was elected to round up several empty cans with which the argument could be settled. I was to set the cans up a proper distance away and the shooters would knock them down from as far back as possible, once and for all buttoning the other's lip while adding considerable bulk to his bank account.

It took me all of two minutes to come up with a dozen or so roadside rejects, and Daddy told me where to put them up, two at a time. "Y'all can start there, then move backwards as you knock 'em down," he told the disagreeing pair.

"Shucks, man, you couldn't hit them cans from here with a bazooka, much less a shotgun," one of them piped up. His motion was quickly seconded by the other.

"Well, I thought y'all had some long-shootin' guns," was the innocent (I guess!) reply. "But if that ain't where you want those cans put, tell him where to start."

Naturally, that response didn't set too well with either of the good ol' boys. The offshoot of their further argument was that Daddy had a standing invitation to join their wager. Nodding slowly and without a word, he pulled out the sixteen-gauge pump and handed it to me.

"Knock them cans down," was all he said. I, knowing better than to disobey, followed orders. It was as simple as that.

After putting up two more in the same place and listening as their twelve-gauges sent pellets resounding a pitiful "tink-tink" off only one of them, I silently became much better acquainted with the late president's greenback cameo.

Later, I was instructed to go pick up one of the mangled cans. The one I selected was gold in color; kind of like the substance our national currency is based upon. For years, Daddy kept that can in the glove box of his pickup, although I could not imagine why.

Along with the paper that had already traded hands, there were some very attractive offers made for a certain Model 12 that day. Daddy would have sooner sold me than that gun. Years later, I found out just how much satisfaction he got from that afternoon, because I had a similar experience.

My number one work gun was for years that birthday present Winchester automatic, the old Model 1400, and has a twenty-six-inch improved cylinder barrel. It's perfect for quail and early-season doves. But it won't kill a bear at a thousand yards, as some hunters would have you believe theirs will. One such guy put the reputation of his thirty-inch, full-choke barrel, twelve-gauge on the line and came away with it severely

sullied. Not quite as much lucre changed hands on this occasion, but it was sweet nonetheless.

Daddy's old pump gun was involved in this contest, too . . .

It had commenced to rain on that second Saturday of dove season, not long after we set up shop around the field. That wasn't really bad news, because the sun had blazed down the week before and made things miserable, just as they had been before the bottom of that day's clouds finally gave out. The dozen or so hunters on my end of the field made for a nearby tractor barn to keep from drowning and maybe down a bit of refreshment while attempting to out-lie the others. Among the first comments was a derogatory one directed at my little auto. I was just too hot to take kindly to the phrasing. Never having possessed the cool-headedness or knowledge of when to keep a shut mouth like Daddy, I couldn't resist the baiting.

"This little gun won't shoot as far as yours, but I happen to know where there's one that will," I gritted.

Think he listened?

"Yeah, but you ain't got it with you, and you can't get to it right now, can you?" came the lashing retort.

"Just happen to have it in a special case in the truck."

Maybe we were both wrong. But hindsight, as they say . . .

At any rate, after a short hike through the rain the pump was pulled from the pickup. Following another walk in the wet, a pair of bottles was perched on a rusty jumble of forgotten tractor parts.

If I and two of my friends who stood beside me at the time recall correctly, at his shot exactly three pellets grazed the bottle on the left.

"We'll move up three steps after you shoot," came the smug statement as he rammed home another shell.

"Think you just burned your bacon, Hoss," I replied, the sting of his prodding still sharp.

As I stepped to the boot-toe mark in the mud where he had stood, I could clearly see those two shooters of years before.

That ugly gold can also came to mind for some reason. Index-fingering the safety off, there was no doubt what was about to happen. With my first shot, glass shattered, and my ex-buddy's bottom lip dropped down around his hips. We went no further, other than a brief trip later to make a deposit.

He stands way down the dove field from me these days, and on the other side if he can find a spot there. There's really no reason for that, because I can't hit birds too far away. My range isn't the gun's fault, but he apparently doesn't realize that. And by the way, just in case you decide to pull something out of the glove box in my truck, take care. There's been a couple of small pieces of broken glass in there for years . . .

AMONG THE OTHER SHOTGUNS I'VE HAD THE PLEASURE, OR LACK THEREOF, of owning over the years was one I took with me for the first time one afternoon as I shot birds with Walter Foy. Travis Davis, a bear of a man, a heck of a good friend, and a thirty-year educator who had recently gotten out of the business, was also along. They were at the other end of the field from me to begin with, a fact I became very appreciative of. We later closed up, a mistake that won't be repeated.

As I sat in my own little corner of the world, dove after dove rushed merrily by, thanking me for the cooling, lead-spawned breezes I was directing their way. Yessir, all my gun needed was twirling blades and light bulbs and it could have easily passed for a decorative ceiling fan. My two compadres were busy embarrassing the blue blazes out of me by missing once or twice an hour. I continued to pile up hulls by the case and meatless feathers by the pillow. Thinking man that I am, I commenced to reason all this out.

For starters, there was no doubt that the shotgun was the culprit. The particular model I was holding happened to be a sixteen-gauge relic dropped, probably on purpose, by one of Columbus' explorers. I had recently purchased it from one Vito "Scarface" Luccesi for approximately the cost of a space shuttle down payment. The gun would shoot; it would not, however, hit anything flying, running, or otherwise putting distance between it and myself. It would lovingly beat one's shoulder into breakfast oatmeal and weighed only slightly more than your average everyday blacksmith's anvil.

Yeah, it was probably the gun.

On the other hand, I eventually found myself shooting beside . . . and considering shooting at . . . Davis, who was touching off an ancient twelve-gauge Browning that kicks like an army mule. This guy weighed around 250 pounds, and he spent half the afternoon getting up off the canvas after the Browning right-crossed him. Also falling down with monotonous regularity were little gray birds, all around him.

Besides that, crouching fairly close by and laughing all the while was Foy, wreaking havoc with his pet, a twenty-gauge that has been trained not to miss and is completely ignorant concerning the term "recoil." He knocked down a couple that zipped by a mile or so high, and both had been recently cooled down by my ceiling fan/shotgun. Well, to reason this out, a twelve and a twenty were working around me, so maybe it wasn't the gun after all. What about the shell load?

I rolled my own, thank you, and had recently had some problems with the firelock hanging up, so an investigation was launched. Finding no obvious afflictions with the original compound, I beefed things up for the next trip, mainly by increasing the amount of blow-up juice, or smokeless powder, as it is known.

Remember Eddie Munster from 1960's TV? When little Ed would touch off one of his junior scientist experiments, most of a wing of Papa Herman's creepy old house would go up in very black smoke. Well, I felt kind of like Eddie when I touched off the first shell, be it filled with "smokeless" powder or not. I later bequeathed the remainder of those loads to Mr. Luccesi for his personal use and probable permanent impairment. By now, he most likely has a nice set of stitches on his shoulder, or where his shoulder used to be, to match those on his face.

Shells aside, I guess the man behind my gun was the probable cause. Having killed a dove back in '93, I still knew for a fact that I could hit them. Maybe I was shooting behind them. I certainly wasn't shooting beside them, because the birds were beside themselves with laughter. Foy came up with the best explanation for success I had heard to date. Having been complimented on the use of his twenty-gauge, Walt replied, "Well, I've been shooting doves for fifty years, so I guess I should be able to hit them pretty well."

Eureka! Just the solution I had been looking for. Just wait, and mark my words. Thirty years from now, I'll be knocking them down coming and going. But those flying from right to left will probably still be giving me trouble.

7

WATCH OUT FOR THE KID

A friend of mine was relating a story not long ago which included all the prime ingredients for the creation of a new member of that species which has become a boil on the butt of the world: the slob hunter.

It seems my buddy was with a handful of other well-trained shooters who had left a field full of slobs who shot, or shot at, everything in sight, tore up the host farmer's acreage with their four-wheelers, and just generally made nuisances of themselves all around. As bad luck would have it, just as the guys who wanted no part of the proceedings took their leave, up skidded the truck of the irate owner, who instructed them, along with their "friends," never to set foot on his place again.

I've seen this form of behavior many times over the years, as I'm sure you have if you've spent any time at all hunting, or fishing as far as that goes. I believe the key is how, or if, the folks in question were taught to go about their business and pleasure. My early career in dove shooting consisted mostly of sitting, watching, and, at the top of the list, learning. I must inform you, all modesty aside, that I was one of the best retrievers ever whelped. Like any good fetcher of the canine variety, I picked up birds only when I was instructed to and, along the same lines, was trained to hand signals, if you know what I mean.

Believe me, if ever I left early to get a bird and, heaven forbid, happened to turn a second incoming target from a nearby hunter in the process, that meat hook which passed for Daddy's right hand would very swiftly become acquainted with portions of my anatomy best left undescribed. That course of action does tend to get the point across!

On opening day of the season past, I witnessed a youngster who would do well to undergo a crash (nice word) course in this type of training. I go into it here in the hope that somewhere down the line, some father can think long and hard about it and make a decent hunter of his son or maybe even someone else's. After all, we have far too many slobs . . . or "maggots" as one of my game warden friends refers to them . . . as it is.

THERE WERE FOUR OF US ON THIS STEAMY—YOU COULD HAVE BROILED buffalo on my topknot—opening day, and we went to the field early to pick prime spots. The legal shooting hour was high noon, and we were two hours early. As it turned out, we needn't have bothered.

Maybe I should have said "our" season opened at noon, for there was one gun-totin' human . . . I refuse to call him a hunter and indeed question the term "human" . . . who decided the rules didn't apply to him. He will be referred to as The Kid, and was probably twelve to fourteen years old at the time, although how he ever lived to reach that ripe old age is forever beyond me.

There were birds aplenty coming in, and I had been busy taking pictures of doves flying so low and close that they must have been wearing watches. I was eyeball to optics when a thundering shotgun went off fifty feet away. The closest I have ever come to swallowing a Nikon camera complete with two hundred-millimeter-lens was at 11:30 A.M. on that opening day.

After the camera had been pried from my gullet, I was informed that a lone bird had come floating drowsily into the field about ten feet above The Kid's gun barrel. It went up in a cloud of feet, feathers, and little else, out of season and of no use to anyone.

"Come on now," you say, "thirty minutes out of season . . ."

If I, or any of the three with me had done the deed when we were The Kid's age, our guns would probably still be resting shiny-new in their cases and our behinds in plaster casts. That's as it should be. What's wrong is wrong; there is no middle ground here, period and exclamation point. All over the field we could hear mutterings from other hunters thinking the same way. We had all had doves practically lighting on us, but there had been no shooting. Until now.

Even worse was the next episode a few minutes later. And things would degenerate from there. The Kid's second out-of-season bird fell some hundred yards away from the first one . . . and almost in the lap of one of my fellow hunters.

Hundred yards seem like long range for a shotgun to you?

Not really, because The Kid had been traipsing around like Robin Hood and his Merry Men, learning every inch of the field and generally bugging the beetlejuice out of everyone in it. It was like hide-and-seek. Every time one of us would try to get out of his way, he'd pack up and come a'lookin'. I don't know about you, but I'm downright cowardly when it comes to gazing down the barrel of a shotgun being wielded by an under-aged imbecile with glazed eyes.

One of my companions, who almost caught that second dove . . . and with his face no less . . . was so disgusted that he gathered his gear right then and went home without firing a shot. He had raised two sons of his own, both ardent, well-trained hunters. I can still hear him grousing his anger and disbelief.

As you may or may not know, doves develop very definite flight patterns into fields, interrupted seldom and then only by lead shot. Well, The Kid must be destined to become some sort of warped air traffic controller, because he did yeoman duty at picking up and moving to the exact spot where every bird in the field attempted to light or fell, and sending those still flying scattering to Parts Unknown. No, it didn't matter who shot the downed bird, or if that hunter was only ten feet away and had been there since dawn's early light. If a bird fell, The Kid commandeered it.

I remember one episode in which I (finally) snuck far enough away (I thought) from The Kid to bust a high-flying bird. It was hit in the head with a single pellet. I hate to shoot at doves that high, and usually don't, but The Kid had them hugging the clouds by this time. Anyhow, as they often do when hit this way, the bird flared out a single wing and came slowly circling straight down. I couldn't believe my ears, eyes, and blood pressure when the little fool blasted off twice from right behind me, then ran toward the still-falling bird screeching, "Mine! Mine!" at the top of his considerable lungs.

When I had come back to earth after setting a new pole vault record, without a pole, I discovered that his shots had never touched a feather. But he had managed to twang a nerve in a nearby hunter.

"That ain't your bird, boy," the neighbor grunted rather impolitely through clenched teeth. "Get somewhere . . . sit down . . . and stay there."

Forget it; no way was he the kid's kin, who *should* have been peforming this duty. But Neighbor did get the point across, and the budding slob slunk back through the field to sulk. That didn't last long either; within a very few minutes he was back in the mayhem business. And this time, he very nearly got what he deserved.

One of the guys who went to this shoot with me was in his sixties, a rather large person weighing in several ounces over three hundred pounds. The fuse of his temper in no way matched his size, said temper being akin to that of a wolverine with his foot in a steel trap. The big fella was sitting placidly in the shade of a small tree, minding his own business while his head swiveled like an owl's in search of feathered targets. Little did he, or anyone else in the general area, know what was about to happen.

As the warning, "Low bird," came rolling across the field, guess who popped up out of the grass, glazed eyes and all? Big Boy never had a chance as The Kid, about seventy yards away, popped off a load of what must have felt like hyperactive bees through the tree's piddling branches and straight into his massive back.

"THUNDERATION!"

Like a charging bull elephant draped in camouflage, Ol' Big Boy came out from under that tree kicking up a teen-age tornado of dust and flying branches. His unrehearsed (but absolutely magnificent) speech would have blistered the paint off a battleship as he mauled the territory between himself and The Kid, who, for once, was as still as dog days. Perhaps the fact that he was petrified had something to do with the lack of movement.

Those of us who knew the big fella headed him off at the pass and eventually talked him out of murder one, but it was a close thing. Probably the only things that actually prevented a killing was that age had taken a step or two off the older fella's one hundred-yard dash and that The Kid had snapped out of his sudden statue imitation. He then proceeded to remind me of a younger me in a certain especially bullish situation.

By the way, you may be interested in where The Kid's keeper was all this time. He had been planted under another tree with low-hanging branches surrounded by low-life buddies, all the while sipping lager and attempting to believe his own lies. I suppose those limbs kept lead shot from bouncing off his empty skull, which is a real shame.

Even worse, The Kid's behavior will probably continue until someone like Big Boy stomps the fertilizer out of him. Also, in a worst-picture but entirely likely scenario, somebody could very well end up with his brains scattered across an acre or two of corn field, courtesy of guess-who.

I've made light of this situation in some ways, but it really did happen, and a body's getting maimed or killed is not going to be very much fun to a whole lot of people involved. Think about that the next time you take your child out with a deadly weapon. Children look to you for instruction; patience and training can make all the difference between a true hunter and a slob.

8

TOP DOGS

There was one somewhere around your home, probably in a den or dining room. Or maybe it was in the kitchen. Some part of the house had a piece of furniture where you snuggled up and listened at Christmas time, Thanksgiving, reunions, funerals, or any other opportunity when menfolk convened in one end of the local realm and ladies in the other. Needless to say, I never learned a whole lot about quilt-making and proper gossip techniques.

My favorite spots were the kitchen food bar in our house and the front-porch swing at my grandparents'. The elders would spend hours sitting around those oases, drinking coffee by the gallon, their memories walking untold miles of hunting territory from the past. I would be crouched at the foot of that bar or the end of that swing, hanging open-mouthed on every word, thinking to myself that each brush-covered, tree-lined tract of territory they mentioned must be a genuine parcel of paradise.

Over the years since, I've trekked through most of that territory. Looking back on my feelings as a kid, I don't feel the least embarrassed in how naive I might have come across. Because I was right.

Somewhere in those conversations, inevitably, would come a statement that ran something like, "He was the best that ever was." Oh, maybe he would be a she, and maybe it would be the finest quail finder, rabbit trailer, or squirrel sniffer of the century. But when a dog was involved, my ears always perked up just a little higher.

We may as well start with the best that ever was, and don't try to start an argument. Besides, I've seen too many of them—arguments and dogs—and became an accomplished foot stomper and haggler at a very early age.

Her name was Net, and she was a Llewellyn setter among other things, not the least important of which was baby sitter. This was a task she performed admirably, I am told, when I was in diapers. Seems every time I would crawl toward the local highway, with Mama and Daddy all of two feet behind my pointed head, Net would snag me just behind the diaper fold, cloth-only thank goodness, and keep me within the yard-bordering shrubbery. At that point, I would invoke all the gods of the Sioux nation, turning the request up to maximum volume, and rain small-fisted blows about her face and eyes . . . all of which she would duly ignore.

There are many more stories about that dog that you probably wouldn't believe either, but like that one they happen to be true. Mostly, though, she was one jewel of a hunting dog.

There were also some pretty good dogs that ran the clothesline behind my grandparents' place. Ol' Belle, fat and lazy around the yard but a holy terror on brown birds, started things off and later helped to raise and teach two sons we kept out of one of her litters. Jeff was cross-eyed, and worked close; Sport was long-legged and a rangy hunter. One had to keep up with Sport pretty close if he was to be included on the trip home.

My favorite episode involving Net came shortly after Belle's death, with just the aging setter and that pair of younger pointers. Four of us were easing along behind the dogs when we came to a narrow ditch four or so feet deep. A large pile of pine tops from a recent timber cutting had been dumped into the depression. Sport and Jeff sailed over it with nary a thought, and commenced sniffing along the other side. But when Net topped our side, she hit the ground like a poleaxed mule; not exactly pointed, but not moving a hair.

Well, Daddy was ready to hunt on, and not a little embarrassed after the bunch of us walked all over the place with no birds launching into orbit. He gruffly told her to look further. The dog quivered like she had the ague, but that was the only movement we were to get out of her, even after he had scolded her with a couple of very light index finger taps behind the eyebrows. Totally exasperated, he finally picked her up bodily to tote her across the ditch, the rest of us whistling "Dixie" and standing around admiring the tops of our hunting boots all the while.

At that precise moment, the covey of about twenty birds busted out from under the pine tops, leaving our jaws hanging to our belt buckles and our guns cradled uselessly. Until the day he buried her, Daddy never touched that dog again in anger. Sport and Jeff? They got a little talking-to of their own for clearing that ditch, but it was hard to fault the boys. They just weren't the caliber of animal Net was.

If I had to pick a second all-time favorite . . . nobody can have just one . . . it wouldn't take much consideration. Remember that first really good dog of your very own, be it of the hunting or mutt variety? I thought so.

When my Uncle Kermit was killed, he had a beautiful gold-and-white English setter pup just being started in the field. The dog was given to me the second week of August, and I had a mere three months to get him ready for his first full year of quail hunting. That first season was to be pure delight for both us pups.

From day one, intelligence had glowed from his golden eyes. He was small when I first brought him home, and at fifteen years

old, I wasn't exactly the largest kid on the block, either. But the youngster's bone structure gave promise of a tough, muscular champ, something every puny, pre-development, teen-aged boy dreams of becoming.

"Yessir," I firmly resolved, "we'll both be regular hosses."

The training included, if I remember correctly, four "severe" beatings of my pup. These involved rolled-up newspaper shredded at one end and, as you can imagine, the pain inflicted roughly resembled that of a young gnat landing on your fist. The point is that the dog was duly chastised and knew he had made a mistake. This one was smart enough not to repeat it. By the way, it is my firmly-held opinion that treating a dog with love and respect will get you much farther down the training road than will brutality. In other words, treat him right and he'll return the favor.

Nothing has ever amazed me more than the inbred knowledge of a bird dog, and this one only added to that wonder. Think about it. How do you go about teaching a dog to lock up on point when he comes upon a particular covey of birds? How does the dog know whether or not to point robins? Or field larks? What happens when a raucous flock of crows flaps overhead? Should he point then? Just what is it about the bobwhite quail?

Well, whatever it is, this pup had it figured out. His first time in the field was an exercise in which he tagged along behind Uncle Math's beloved pointer, Joe. "They learn best from watching the older ones," Math told me, which sounded awfully familiar when I considered my own teaching.

Problem was, we got into only one covey of birds that frosty morning. Guess which dog ran by the bunch of bobs while ranging merrily on its way, and which one settled into a marble-slab lockup? If I live to be a thousand years old, I'll never forget that morning and that little setter's first point.

He didn't know a thing about style. He could not possibly have cared less where Joe was or what the other dog was doing. All the pup knew was that something from deep down in his soul was beckoning, instructing him to do exactly the right things: stand still and show who fed him where the pottidges were.

It was my first dog's first point; with my first shot, a bird fell.

In spite of the fact that Uncle Math took two with his magic twenty-gauge, the scales were vastly unbalanced; no way would he ever appreciate his double as much as I would my single.

The pointer, Joe, was in the process of going bonkers seconds after our shots sounded. He came flying in to our urgent calls of, "Dead in here. Dead. Dead bird, here. Dead."

But we weren't concerned with Joe at the moment. And if the truth be told, after my little setter got the message and gingerly mouthed his first dead-bird retrieve, dropping it into my quivering hand, I never had much interest in Joe again.

The pup's name was Sam, or Sambo as I usually referred to him, and he was kept in an immaculate chainlink fence pen about fifteen feet wide, thirty feet long, and eight feet high. Mama always said that if I had kept my room as neat as I did Sambo's pen, she'd never have voiced a complaint.

The only times the pup got out was when I exercised him every day after school, and when we went hunting, which was every instant I could get into the woods. We romped together like we were in love, and I wouldn't hesitate to say that this was exactly the case. I had visions of a second season in which we reached that magical, old-time figure of downing two hundred quail, just me and Sambo.

But trouble was brewing.

There came upon the scene another, much larger dog that resembled Sam in color and little else. This newcomer was the neighborhood scourge, trampling our new rental-house neighbor's garden, leaving his stinking calling cards at every opportunity, scattering trash, howling at the moon, and generally refining himself to becoming a perfect pain in the butt, at which he had considerable natural talent. He was a good-looking dog and his ramblings didn't bother me all that much, so I allowed him to go on about his business. That, as it turned out, was a terrible mistake.

Not long after that first hunting season ended, just before my senior year of high school was over, I walked out back one morning en route to my car. (In case you're wondering, $54.29 a month, paid for by Yours Sweatily compliments of Theo Gay Construction!) As always, I whistled to Sam, who was lying in front of his private apartment complex. He did not respond.

Second time, same result. This wasn't like him, so I went to investigate, only to find him dead.

School, as you may imagine, was out for the day.

I won't go into deep, painful detail here, but cradling Sam gently, I washed him one last time. With tears, no less, which is something no self-respecting, high school senior male would ever be caught doing under any circumstances. Later, after Daddy had literally dragged me away from my first real love, we took Sambo to the local vet, who confirmed our suspicions: he had been poisoned, as helpless as an animal could possibly be, in his own pen.

Besides being an obvious prize, Sam was the last link I had to my beloved Kermit, and I must admit that I wasn't handling that particular loss very well, either, at the time.

I will always believe that the worthless old so-and-so who lived next door, probably mistaking the two dogs, killed mine out of the blackness of his heart. I do know for a fact that two days after I found Sambo, Daddy brought up the situation in sideyard conversation.

A word of warning may be in order here, but it is what it is. My daddy was a plain man, keeping mostly to himself. But when his boys were involved, certain characteristics of highly-agitated grizzly would evolve from beneath his quiet demeanor. I have boys; go messing with them and the wolf in me comes out. I understand.

But during that chat over the shrubbery dividing our two yards, I believe homicide was mentioned if certain pertinent facts involving poison were ever uncovered. Within a week, the renter had packed up his belongings and gotten out of the neighborhood. So what do you think?

I've had many other dogs since, some good, some worthless. But Ol' Sambo? I miss him still.

THE RABBIT DOG MAN

Everybody should have a friend like J. T. Turner. You know somebody like him, somebody who makes this old world a better place just by being in it; who brings a smile to one's face on sight; a person whose innate good humor and easygoing ways put folks instantly at ease. I'm a people person, so let me tell you a mite about the man and then we'll get into a story or two about him and some of the finest rabbit dogs that ever jumped off a tailgate.

Tee, as he is most often called, hailed from Ft. Payne, Alabama, a small town in the mountainous northern region of that state. It's a simple place, much like the one I was raised in, and Tee is a man of simple pleasures. Among them are a family that would make any man proud and his hunting and fishing.

Along that line there are his "babies." I have never seen a man treat beagle hounds with so much love and tenderness, then turn right around and do his dead-level best to run the legs off of them! There was one special trip when I hunted with

53

Tee during which he ran five dogs. He described them as . . .
are you ready for this? . . . "the best I've ever had."

Over the years, I've walked behind quite a few rabbit
dogs, and Tee knew it. For him to make such a qualifying
statement took a close friend to hear; the man does not
boast. There was seldom a slouch in any of his previous
bunches, but I would have to agree with his latest assess-
ment. The only way to get those dogs off a hot rabbit trail
was to either kill the rabbit and show it to 'em, proving that
they had wrapped up a job well done, or catch the dogs by
hand, which is not exactly the most enjoyable of pastimes.

For a while, Tee was splitting up his living quarters
between Ft. Payne and my hometown, located farther south
and just about always hotter temperature-wise. His heart,
you see, sometimes tocks when it should be ticking, slowing
him down a bit. Sweltering heat is not in his best interest in
summer, nor is bitter cold in winter. So he summered there
in the cool of the hills and wintered, thankfully, near me
from about September on through rabbit season.

A while back, after having been away up north and
greatly missed, Tee came down from the mountains to renew
old acquaintances, including me and several members of the
family Leporidae. We had been aching to get together, shotguns in hand. Come go with us . . .

HIS PIERCING BLUE EYES, FULL OF LAUGHTER AND HIDING MORE THAN A
double dose of life's hardship and pain, lit up as I stepped
out of the truck. I know mine did, too. There is no awkward-
ness among old friends, and even though we haven't seen
each other for too long, we pick up right where we left off.
We're going hunting together; that makes up for lost time.

The narrow, muddy field road before us is surrounded by
thick brush and head-high pines. The two hundred or so
acres we're going to hunt hide spots that would stall a Tiger
tank, but that doesn't matter. The pushed-up brush piles
and nearly-impenetrable stands of briars are like rabbit

condos. We plan to visit every one of them along the way.

Pleasantries are exchanged, briefly, between us. The dogs, bellowing their indignation at being kept locked in the home-made truck box, are turned out. Piling off the back of the old pickup, they commence to check out the leavings of every member of the canine family that has passed through the area in the last hundred years, then make sure the next generation will have the same opportunity. But less than three minutes after the hounds are loosed and following a little booted impetus from the gent who buys their feed, they set up a cacophony that makes the hair along the back of a hunter's neck stand up.

Comes the sudden realization that it has been too long since I've heard that sound, and I vow now not to let so much time between concerts pass by again. The rabbit the dogs have jumped is off to the races. There is only one thing for me to do: head him off.

Humping it down an old logging road through the thick stuff, I suddenly realize from the sound of the pack that the cottontail has turned. Stand still; be quiet; wait. He's pulling that favorite trick of heading right back to where he started, although it may be a mile or two round-trip. But the dogs are getting closer now, pushing him hard. He hasn't been shot at, so he's worrying about what's behind, not ahead. Just wait. Do not move.

At this point, the quarry is in no mood for lolly-gagging. He has been doing his best to put a couple of zip codes between himself and the beagles, but they're closing in and would enjoy nothing more than some rather rare hare for snack time.

Watch careful now. He can crossroad before you can say it.

The bushes off to the right shiver a bit. No wind. Dog? No baying.

The flash of brown streaks into the logging trail even as the scattergun is swinging itself automatically into position. There

is no time to aim, as if one aimed a shotgun anyway. I point it and squeeze the trigger. The roar of the Model 12 bounces off the pines ahead, and suddenly all is still.

There are, after all, few things quieter than a dead rabbit.

The dogs, hearing the shot, come a'running. I hold their quarry up and let them admire it a bit. Praise 'em, even brag on 'em a little. And then mercilessly send them on their way. Run them 'til their tails are swollen and bloody, their pads slashed and tender, bodies aching from exertion and tongues hanging out to prove it. Because I know that if it is at all possible the babies love it even more than I do.

"You git 'im?" Tee's nasal twang reverberates through the brush. As I reply in the affirmative, there's only a brief chuckle, then a hearty, "Hurry, babies. Ain't got no rabbits under our feet. Git out there and look. Hurry, babies. Hurry."

They do, and we do. We follow the dogs through open fields, across narrow dirt roads, and through briars that we'll think more about tonight when we get a good look at all the puncture wounds in our carcasses. No time for that now, though.

Lug those heavy, mud-caked boots over long-forgotten fences, beaten down by time and sinking into the ever-weaving vines and reeds. Tote that gun carefully; never know when it might be needed in a split-second. Think about how I've always wanted to deer hunt back in here but have never seen the inside of the place because it was too thick looking from the outside.

And all this for a rabbit and a dog. And maybe a laugh or two. Like when Tee steps over the bank of a small creek and into a stump hole, nearly dropping out of sight: "How deep does holes grow around here?" he cracks.

Or when I miss a cottontail and have to put up with the return ribbing, then laugh at myself. That's all right; his time will come.

Two brief afternoons we had. Eighteen rabbits and ten times as many jaunts through that prickly stuff for us to run 'em down. But they're now swimming in that thick gravy, and it has been two good days with old Tee and the babies.

They just don't make enough of those days to go around.

10

THE SQUIRREL DOG

There once was a very different type of creature, a mytho-
logical one I always believed, than the dogs we were
always tripping over around the homestead. It was known as a
squirrel dog, and I had heard stories about it for years.

Any high-IQ member of the squirrel dog species would
sniff out a nut-chewing rodent's tracks on the ground and
chase the little bugger up a tree, never making a sound until
all was set for whoever followed the dog to come and collect
the prize. At that point, with his quarry perched up a hickory
and the gun-totin' master humpin' it into sight, the canine
would commit vocal murder while attempting to climb the
proper tree.

The collection process was accomplished in fine fashion,
as I recall, with a .22 single-shot rifle and never anything else.
Shotguns were considered not at all sporting. The squirrel
would be neatly clipped behind the ears with never more than
one .22 Short and promptly come tumbling down like a hairy
rock. It would then be gathered up by the dog, which used

nothing but gums to pick up the late, lamented rodent and drop it at his master's feet.

All this made for a fine story, but I had never actually seen a real, live-and-in-person squirrel dog until recently. Oh, I had propped my peepers on some that were reportedly among the very best, but once they got into the woods they didn't seem to know squirrels from hickory nuts.

The animal that I was recently introduced to was named Princess. She was a white bulldog, and looked as if she could gnaw the kneecaps off a sasquatch without breaking a sweat. We are talking about one large dog, and while we are, please allow me to leave Princess (which I did in one heck of a hurry upon first impression as she lumbered off the back of a pickup and toward me!) for a moment of discussion on what I thought a real squirrel dog should look like. Also included is one of the most uproarious episodes involving canines that I have ever witnessed.

FOR SOME REASON OR OTHER, I HAD ALWAYS PICTURED A SQUIRREL DOG as something of the feist variety, or maybe a beagle, size and temperament-wise. Although we did a lot of squirrel hunting around the farm via still-hunting and stalking, the major reason I never asked for a squirrel dog to go along with our setters, pointers, and bulldogs was that it is my personal belief that a feist dog is about as useless as teats on a bull.

That is purely personal opinion, and you feist lovers don't begin addressing your hate mail just yet; it gets worse.

The only feist I know of that ever did any semblance of a good deed . . . which involved my nearly busting a gut laughing at a situation that probably wasn't funny at all . . . was one of a pair belonging to a local woman and her truck-driver husband. The couple owned a place that Daddy and I were re-roofing when I first went to work with him.

Despite the fact that I was a teenager and had been around all types of dogs all my life, I had only been bitten twice. Both times were by feists. The word "feisty" is defined as "touchy; quarrelsome" in my dictionary, and you can imagine where it came from. A feist dog usually fits that bill perfectly.

The woman we were working for had the gall to tell us that those dogs of hers would sometimes even bite her husband when he came off the road from a long haul! That remark did nothing to especially endear either the woman or the dogs to me, but it did account for quite a few sideways glances as I lugged stuff through the place. What did convince me that I had finally seen the proverbial only good feist was the day one of them took his last bite.

It happened on a typical July afternoon in Georgia, 100 degrees on the ground, 130 or better on the roof. We were working in shifts, because it was dangerous to carry buckets of tar or drive nails for too long a time in such heat. This type weather does wonders for one's metabolism when he considers the fact that he's getting ahead in the world at the rate of a buck-fifty an hour. Along about three o'clock, the most murderous hour of all, a halt had been called for the both of us, and we were in the blessed shade of the screened-in back porch.

As I recall, the woman was discussing extending the job and doing the porch's roof, too. Naturally, I was just thrilled as all get-out at this prospect while lounging in a corner and eyeing those feists. They, in turn, seemed to be looking at my ankles with more than casual interest. Let 'em look. I was wearing my hunting boots which were also my work boots, not to mention the only boots in my possession.

"Yeah baby," I was thinking as they sized me up, "if you come for my hide, all you're gonna get is a steel-reinforced toe in the chops."

Who knows? Maybe they were thinking the same thing.

My dad always wore brogan work shoes on the job, and the dogs would cast occasional drooling glances at them, also. One major problem, though, was that Daddy had a habit of using his claw hammer as a pointer while talking, gesturing at this or that as the discussion went on. Right now, the hammer was, as always, waving to and fro. Alas, along about the middle of the conversation, a certain four-legged idiot totally lost his mind, took it upon himself to sidle up uninvited from behind, and sink his teeth to the gums just above Daddy's shoe tops.

He shouldn't have done that.

Reflex took over, I suppose, and with a brief sentence featuring some quite impressive blue thunder, the hammer that had driven thirty or forty million nails came flashing down. As usual, it didn't miss what it was swung at. The dog's reaction was much like he had been struck by lightning. He never moved again, except for the four or so feet he covered courtesy of the hammer's momentum.

Thunderstruck, I felt intense weakness to the point of falling to my knees in uncontrollable laughter. It just happened so fast!

Seconds later, with the other feist wisely making himself as small as possible under the nearest available chair, the woman was hysterical. And so was I, although our tears were flowing from very different ends of the emotional spectrum. Up until that thirteenth year of my life, that was probably the funniest thing I ever saw, and it still ranks pretty high. Maybe you just had to be there to appreciate the suddenness of it, or maybe you need a death wish for feists. But my ribs were sore for days after I had run off that porch to escape Daddy's scathing glare.

The crowning blow came when the husband, not due in from somewhere or other for a couple of days, came rolling up mere minutes after the dog had turned up his toes. Upon hearing the tearful details, he pulled Daddy . . . who was over the pain of being bitten, mortified at what he had done in the blink of an eye, and madder'n the dickens at me for laughing about it . . . aside and informed him that he would tack another hundred onto the roof job if he took care of the other feist before we left. That broke the ice somewhat, tickled Daddy a tad, and probably saved my life.

Don't get me wrong; nobody loves dogs more than I do. Put in a couple million training hours with good working dogs like I have and a man can't help but love them. But feists? Where's my hammer?

Getting back, at last, to Princess, I should have known that my old buddy Tee Turner had a squirrel dog. After all, with rabbit dogs, coon dogs . . . you name it, Tee has it. And he quickly proved that this latest assertion concerning the big pooch was no tall tale, although I have blind faith in pretty much anything he says.

"I just put her out in a holler and sit and listen," he informed me. "When she's got one treed, she lets me know. It's just right hunting small hollers for the dog and two hunters. With two, you can chase the squirrel around from one side of the tree to the other when it hides from the first one of us it spots. A squirrel will flatten himself out on a limb, too, but one of the two guys just about always gets a shot."

Less than five minutes later, after we had walked less than fifty yards, Princess proved her worth. She put the first squirrel up there, and over the next thirty minutes treed eight more. We killed six of those, and covered less than five hundred yards of territory in the process.

As Tee said, "The thing I like about this kind of hunting is that you don't have to kill yourself walking doing it."

Oh yeah, Virginia, there is a squirrel dog. I still have trouble believing it's a big ol' white bulldog . . . but at least it's not a feist.

THERE WAS ANOTHER EXCUSE FOR A CANINE, THIS ONE SOMEWHAT LARGER than a feist, that I became acquainted with a couple of years later. While he looked absolutely nothing like a feist, it was obvious from the outset that his brain closely resembled that of one. I'm tellin' you, that was one stupid . . . or ill-trained . . . piece of dog.

"Joooooooooe!!!" The scream bounced off the pines in echo for perhaps the hundredth time that morning, the big black Labrador retriever paying no more attention than he had the previous ninety-nine. Somebody, no matter who, had shot down a bird, and he was going to fetch it, his master's voice be hanged. Speaking of masters, we never did figure out who was training whom.

The doves had been flying sporadically, it was hotter than fresh lava and tempers were short. Fittingly, this was the same dove field in which The Kid had narrowly escaped the hiding of his life. It was a given that something amiss was about to happen.

A gentleman on a nearby stand was settled in with a gorgeous golden retriever, and since the birds were few and far between, I went over to express my admiration. We got to talking about the big Lab, and wound up assessing his IQ at about one-half on a scale of one to a hundred.

The bird that had been blasted happened to be the third shot down by a humble-appearing elderly gent decked out in well-worn, Pointer-brand overhauls and squatting some fifty yards from me. The dog had filched all three, and despite the fact that the owner had returned the first two and was en route to doing so with the third, it was clear that the older fellow was more than a little displeased.

Now I happen to have a weak spot for folks like that old man, because it is your obedient servant's opinion that they make up the prime kind of glue that holds this egg shell world together. Like Daddy, they very seldom say more than they mean or fail to mean exactly what they say, and this gent was no exception. I knew something pretty interesting was coming, and so eased over to within eavesdropping range, maybe heading off an execution or two in the process.

"I just don't know what I'm going to do about that dog," Owner was lamenting. "I've worked with him and worked with him, and just can't seem to be able to get him to mind."

The old man rubbed his grizzled jaw a second or two, then out it came. I had thought myself prepared to head off a repeat performance of Day of the Feist, but once again I was rendered laughingly helpless by the suddenness of the retort.

"Tell ya what ya do," he drawled, fingering his overhaul galluses with one hand, tenderly cradling a Model 12 that I would have given the ranch for with the other. "Go on out to Kmart and git you a pair of them heavy cowhide boots with the thick lug soles on 'em. Put 'em on, tie 'em up real tight, git a good holt on that dog's collar, and then stomp the soles off them boots on that idiot's hide. He's apt to pay a little more mind to you afterward."

While it didn't appear overly funny to the man with the dog, I thought I'd bust. Old Man shuffled back to his stand, obviously in a much better frame of mind, and Owner, er, um, "escorted" Joe right on to the truck, giving me a look like he probably wouldn't vote for me in the next election. But as far as that afternoon went, things sure flowed smoother; at least after I got the dirt off my hands and knees and the tears out of my eyes.

11

RABBITS AND DEER
DON'T MIX

Somewhere down the line, we're going to get into that bane of outdoors writers everywhere: How To Harvest The Whitetail Deer Each And Every Time I Want To, Even If It Means Shooting It Through The Kitchen Window With A Pellet Pistol.

But before we do, we must pay our dues. In other words, we should learn how NOT to do so. Tee is going to help us.

Although you will recall he has some of the finest rabbit-running beagles you will ever hope to listen to in a race, don't ever forget that Murphy's Law extends well into rabbit season. I well remember the first time we took Tee's dogs out: Peaches, the best ever; Big Ruby and Little Ruby; Ginger, Doc, and a couple of first-timers enrolled in class.

Ol' Tee's two sons, Chris and Dennis, were with us this time. Dennis was a yonker of about fifteen years, Chris probably twenty or so at the time. Chris was also roughly the size of half a double-wide mobile home, so not many folks argued with him. Tee, however, who is definitely not the shy type, shared no such compunctions and especially when it came to his dogs.

"Hurry babies," he encouraged as we followed their busy noses and busier tails through the thick stuff that morning. "Hurry. Heeeee, heeeeee, yiiiiii on there."

Don't ask me, but the dogs understood perfectly.

Shortly after Tee's caressing calls came that gorgeous, lilting, hyperactive bawl that lets a hunter know the chase is on. Fourteen circular miles later, all of them spent getting acquainted with bamboo and briars within the same two-hundred-acre tract of land, Chris hollered, "Daddy, the dogs are running a deer over here across the swamp."

"Naaaawww," came the reply. "You know my dogs don't run no deer."

"Well, I reckon I see it, and they're right behind it!"

Well, Tee had to see it too, if he was to believe it, so off we set.

About the time we had finished slogging to the spot where what sounded like a minor-league train wreck was in progress, a doe that must have weighed two hundred pounds piled out right on top of us. And there was a beagle pup yapping at each of her heels.

Without blinking an eye, Turner gave me his best down-home Alabama glare and said, "Blast if y'all ain't got the biggest rabbits I've ever seen."

That was all well and good, but we still had to either kill the "rabbit" or catch the puppies, so off I went to waylay 'em. Minutes later, their tone, as well as direction, changed, so off to a nearby pasture I hustled, shell-filled camo bouncing and scattergun held high. Crossing a fence that separated the neighboring pasture plot from our hunting territory and hunkering down beside the rusting wire, I waited only briefly before, sure enough, here came the second train wreck.

As my eyeballs were in the process of putting on admirable extra weight and circumference, one of the nicest bucks I have ever seen soared over the fence not thirty feet away, every rippling muscle outlined as if in slow motion . . . in which the whitetail definitely was not. Evidently, he had been laying low

all the while and the youngsters happened to stumble onto him, decide he would be easier to catch than the doe they'd been chasing, and bring the rest of the pack over with their juvenile baying.

Needless to say, I was dumbfounded, but snapped back to reality when the full chasing crew arrived. In the darnedest tangle of yapping and snapping beagles you will hopefully never see, they piled full tilt into the fence, one atop the other. I could see, not to mention hear, with crystal clarity that the pooches up front did not at all appreciate their brethren and sistren piling in from behind. Wading in with an uh, er, "quaint" whispered admonition or two, I finally got them separated, losing only parts of several fingers in the process.

Yessir, we've got some big rabbits down here; smart ones, too.

12

GETTING STARTED WITH SQUIRRELS

R abbits," as they say in my part of the pasture, "is fine, but so is squirrels." And we had to eat, thus we had to hunt, years before I ever lucked onto Princess. Therefore, let us backtrack in time . . .

It is pretty much a ritual that boys down South earn their way into a dove field or into the back seat of an old hunting car headed into quail territory by first outsmarting and ambushing "any of various arboreal rodents of the genus Sciurus, and related genera, usually with gray or reddish-brown fur and a long, flexible, bushy tail."

The dictionary that provided that illustrious introduction to ol' bushytail didn't mention the fact that he can also run like a ticked-off racehorse and climb faster than a monkey chasing low-flying bananas.

You may remember from earlier accounts, and may understandably have attempted to forget, the names Jerry and Glynn. Both were members of my family, so to speak, one in fact and the other a boon companion that my parents could never seem to get rid of. Nor could his.

At various times, it all worked out for the best, especially when the three of us huddled to consider what was on the various supper tables each night and to decide which one we would surround like Commanches, forks and knives in hand.

Many times, those tables would feature squirrel meat. In fact, we ate so much squirrel that to this day Jerry loves a hickory nut better'n sirloin, but then Jerry always was just off the beaten path. My preference for raw pecans over grilled T-bone has nothing whatever to do with that early upbringing. To be perfectly and uncategorically honest, I'm basically a vegetarian anyway. (That sudden crash was our best Sunday plates hitting the floor; my spouse momentarily lost her grip.)

Anyhow, if any of you live in the United States, there is the distinct possibility that you have become acquainted with that roadside piece of heaven known as "Stuckey's." Mr. W. S. Stuckey, the founder of that candy-selling chain, lived most of the long years of his life, which included the first few and very formative of mine, in a big white house a short piece from our'n. In front of his home was located the only traffic light in Eastman, Georgia. That's how big Mr. Stuckey, bless him, was.

Stuckey's has sold and still sells some of the finest candy you'll ever salivate over. Two of its basic ingredients are chocolate and pecans. Melt down all the chocolate in Stuckey's candy sold over the years and you'd have enough to plaster over every crater on Jupiter.

Unfortunately, we couldn't help you much with the chocolate end of it, but Eastman and Dodge County had a heckuva heap of pecan trees when I was coming up. Know what else likes pecans? That's right: squirrels.

Probably the very first actual hunting lesson that I ever learned . . . and this is not to be confused with gun safety lessons, which were considered much more important . . . came on my initial trip to a grove of Mr. Stuckey's pecan trees. We hunted the grove as well as wooded areas which bordered it on three sides. There was a busy highway on the other. To this day, regardless of what I go into the treeline after, I consider this lesson the single most important factor in a successful hunt. Look back with me and think on it. You probably learned much the same way.

IT'S COLD. HARD COLD. IF SOMEBODY THUMPED MY EARS FROM BEHIND, there'd be a heck of a brawl. Luckily, nobody is around but Daddy, and he ain't in a thumping mood. Jerry and his pa are a hundred yards or so off through the trees.

Ice crunches underfoot as we make our way down through the eerie pecan trees in the dark, wondering where this cold came from all of a sudden. The trees are suffering. I think about the small-time tree owners. Pecans make good Christmas money. What will the presents look like this year, and will there be any at all after next growing season?

"What about being quiet?" The shush snaps me back to earth.

"Don't stomp," Daddy hisses. "Walk on the outsides of your boots, and ease 'em down. Any time you go into the woods, you disturb things, especially little things. They spread the word to everything else. It doesn't matter what you're hunting; if you go stomping in like a gorilla, you won't find it. Thing that lives in the woods, it knows what's going on all the time; if something's out of place or something big comes crashing into its world, a wild thing gets quiet and disappears. You can forget hunting when that happens."

Sound familiar? File it away. Trust me, I learned it in a large hurry.

With the breaking of first light, thirty minutes later, the world wakes up. First thing out and about is the squirrel, and his barking alarm clock kicks off everything else. You have to get up pretty early in the morning . . .

Cuss, but it's cold. Little breeze getting up really helps things . . . like hypothermia, for example. No way to put my bare (forgot the gloves again!) hand on that ice-blue shotgun barrel. That's right, shotgun. The old hands with their great squirrel dogs could use rifles if they wanted to, but I like my odds with the scattergun much better.

Oh well, shudder and wait, shudder and . . .

What was that movement?

There are nests off to the right, three of them in a pair of oaks, and something has caught my eye. The first squirrel comes slipping down, a foot at a time and stops, looking around . . . for me . . . then scats another ten or so inches. It's so quiet, thanks mainly to the fact that I'm frozen to the stump, that he never has a clue.

BOOOOMMM. There's nothing quite so sweet as the sound of a shotgun blast in the cold gray mist. Settle on back. Remember the lesson, because the whole world's now deathly still again. Give them five more minutes to calm down and open up shop a second time. Then I'll repeat the process. And do it again . . .

SO THAT WE DON'T HAVE FAR TO TRAVEL, LET US SLIP A COUPLE HUNDRED yards, nearly a year and seventy degrees Fahrenheit forward in that same head of woods. This time, we are not planted in the ground waiting on something to come down. Rather, we are easing along looking for movement, same four of us spread out and wary, two each, father and son, side-by-side. And instead of cold, it's hot: sweating, sitting-down-resting, big-mosquito hot.

In other words, it's snake weather.

The phrase "looking for movement" carries quite a different connotation this time of year than it did back in the dead of winter. One advantage the cold does provide is the absence of vegetation, which means there are fewer hiding places for what we'll be shooting at, providing we find it. Then too, cold-blooded snakes are for the most part listless at that time.

On the other hand, finding bushytails at all among the green stuff of the South's late summer and early fall season

is a basic problem. Worst of all, though, there are creepy-crawly things around.

This trip was a meat expedition, nothing else. Unfortunately, it was my meat that was almost chomped upon. I can recall it in slow-motion VistaVision; the entire, haunting episode remains crystal clear. Let's move off quietly into the trees.

It has been raining the past few days and the swamp is pretty bad. A man can move silently on the damp ground underfoot, but visibility in the hardwood tops is almost non-existent. The trick is to strike a happy medium, slow steps to a crawl and look up. If a squirrel spots you, he'll likely run for cover. A favorite trick is to put a large tree between him and the hunter. But with two-man teams, one shooter on each side, somebody usually gets a shot. It takes a sharp eye, a split-second decision, and precise pellet placement to bring him down. When it happens, this is exciting hunting

By the way, did I say "look up?" Pardon me; this is one rule I learned the hard way.

The back side of Daddy's fist and forearm hit me just as I picked up a foot to clear a tangle of cypress roots. Even as precious breath left, I instinctively gasped for more, which would not come. That the solitary thought which crossed my mind as I went down was to point the gun barrel away from my body and his still amazes me.

"BOOM, LOOKOUT, BOOM, BOOM," came all at once.

I was flat on my back, scared spitless, unable to breathe or move, wondering if World War III had just broken out and what I did to start it. That's when the cottonmouth moccasin, as big around as your forearm if you ain't puny, came writhing crazily across my feet and lower legs.

Believe me, it is a terrible feeling to be unable to move, even to breathe, and feel that at any second you are about to be bitten by one of the South's most feared poisonous snakes. About all I can equate it to is the helplessness of a nightmare: running and running, terrified yet unable to escape.

Fortunately for me, the snake was missing about a foot, including head and fangs, of his former self. Thank you very, very much, Mr. Winchester. As close calls come, that one was a tree trunk short.

Daddy, walking maybe two feet ahead of me at the time, later said that the snake was coiled and ready for my lumbering butt as I came around the opposite side of that cypress. Easing through the woods . . . like I should have been doing . . . he had slipped up on that big deadly rascal. It had simply sighted in on the wrong target.

When it was all over, his buddy's yell came rolling though the woods. "Get one?"

"Oh, yeah, I got one."

I agreed. Funny, but I don't remember how many squirrels we took on that trip.

On the other hand, I recall the exact number harvested on a jaunt into the Ocmulgee River swamp when I was fifteen. My Uncle Math was the instructor in this class, and never a better tracker or teacher was born.

Math McCrackin, just so you stay in touch, was my grandmother's brother. His wife, Georgia Eva Mae . . . Aunt Mae . . . was Granddaddy's sister.

She had been blind since the first year of their marriage, which never seemed to jive with the fact that she cooked the best fried chicken in the family. I, also, can cook. In fact, I can whip you up a gospel bird that'll have you coming to our place with the preacher at least every other Sunday. But please do not ask me how it came to be that a woman who cannot tell whether it is light or dark in a room can turn chicken at precisely the proper times, then put it on a platter at its crispiest and best.

Math and Mae used annual bumper crops of love to deal with her blindness, and raised two children along the way. Math also took me under his wing when it came to woods ways. What Mae couldn't see, Math definitely could, and vice versa. He could read the woods like I read books and he also had a very different side. Uncle Math, you see, was the family comedian. Which reminds me . . .

"SQUIRREL . . . POSSUM . . . COON . . . BOBCAT."

Math was steadily walking, pointing and whispering, identifying every piece of track in the swamp. It got more and more interesting to a goggle-eyed teenager as the tracks got bigger. I was to the point of being absolutely amazed and nearly ready to appear so stupid as to ask questions when he nonchalantly rolled off the word, "Snake."

You never knew with Math. Laughing it off, I figured in a split second of mid-stride and sheer ignorance that he was pulling another of his infamous practical jokes. But the ground under the downstroke of my step wasn't quite kosher. In fact, it was moving.

They say that when them big rockets go off down at Cape Kennedy the whole state of Florida shakes. I 'spect it got rocked a little that morning, too, when my boot made contact with the reptile in question.

Math does have his good points, by the way, numbering one and two as near as I can figure. For starters, he's short, at least as compared to me. Then too, he has good ol' broad shoulders. I leaped upon those shoulders en route to the top of a nearby sweet gum, from which I surveyed the general area milliseconds after his initial observation.

Let us not leave out the fact that over the entire, though brief, elapsed time, my vocal chords were exercising themselves on an octave somewhere between Slim Whitman and a champion Swiss yodeler. Math's were busy, too, as he cussed the bluing off his shotgun barrel in a vain attempt to get me to shaddup.

Eventually, he succeeded. I was talked down the slick, now barkless tree only after he explained that the reptile had either been cussed to death or met its demise at the sound of my crystal-shattering screeches.

When the siege was over, Math realized that he had not been bitten, at least not by the snake, and was not dying after all. Discovering that I was in like condition, he was less than pleased. But we still had what was left of four squirrels in hand, and Uncle Math finally became slightly amused at the entire episode.

The humor was evidenced several years later, however.

SNAKES ARE NOT THE ONLY SWAMP CREATURES THAT TEND TO PUT ONE'S metabolism into overdrive. There was a trip with a distant uncle of mine . . . who threatened me with severe bodily harm if I mentioned this episode, thus the reason he is distant . . . where we were split up and I was more than a little lost.

Around home, other kinfolk had tried to lose me on many occasions, so that was old hat. But this tract was sixty miles or so from there, way up north near Macon. Having a magnificent sense of direction . . . which involves standing pat and bellowing up to 6.5 on the Richter Scale until the loser gives up and comes to retrieve the losee . . . I held due course, secure in the knowledge that we would meet up at the car in no more than a minute or so.

As it happened, we ran up with each other a little before that when I saw Uncle James streaking rather awkwardly across the holler and hollerin' like a hellcat. Flagging him down, which was no easy task, I agreed to assist in finding his wallet.

We never did.

I'll always believe it came out as he tried to swim the creek, because the current was pretty swift where he went in. Funny thing, but I could have sworn he'd make it across that slick log he was running on. Hindsight factored in, however, it's true that I didn't take into consideration that he was holding up his pants with one hand and swatting yellow jackets with the other.

He knew as well as I did that these pesky insects are solitary creatures and don't like to be disturbed, especially by objects that smell slightly less than perfumy falling on their log homes. We won't go into exactly how they were disturbed, or how Uncle James came to be holding his pants up, because it's really not that interesting. I do remember that I had taken seven squirrels this time out. James, for some reason, didn't kill any, at least not with his shotgun.

We never found that, either.

13

PROPER TECHNIQUES FOR RABBIT STOMPIN'

I f you have come to the conclusion that we are jumping around from doves to quail to rabbits to squirrels and back again, reach over and pat yourself on the back. This will be accomplished much easier if you have ever shot the likes of a certain shotgun we became acquainted with earlier. In fact, if that criterion has been met, you will probably be able to pull a large portion of your back around to your front, simplifying the task even more.

Hopping from, and coming down hard on, one species to another is exactly what we did as kids. When Grandma made the offhand statement that she "shore would like to have a mess of fried rabbit for supper," half a regiment of my under-aged neighborhood lunatic friends would take her to heart and hit the woods like lemmings into the surf. It was the same with squirrel, fairly easily obtained even for the novice . . . and we have been called worse. "The more the merrier" is a popular phrase in some circles; but there are times . . .

As you may have noticed from personal observance, "friends" can provide invaluable assistance to almost any would-be shooter of supper. Take, for example, a hunter of deer . . . just to graduate to something large . . . stalking his quarry.

The buck has been spotted just beyond certain-sure shooting range, ghosting through the trees and providing a glimpse of a huge palmated hatrack every quarter mile or so. But all is almost in position now; another thirty feet and all the whitetail's earthly problems will be o'er. At that point, the hunter can depend on his companion to enter stage right and make slightly more noise than a cadre of carpenters constructing a cathedral.

Thanks to his friend, the hunter gets a solitary, freshly-harvested-pasture-perfect look at the buck, which will never be less than a twelve-pointer, as it merrily makes its way toward the Grand Tetons.

But there is another manner of hunting at which friends of this type truly and particularly excel. In fact, it seems to bring out the fiend in friend. Yessir, heavy-footed buddies are at their dead-level best when it comes to stompin' for rabbits.

If you have never partaken of rabbit stompin', a quick explanation is in order here. First off no dogs, such as beagles, are allowed. After all, with beagles around, there's a possibility that somebody might actually get a decent shot at a rabbit. As we shall see, that is not the object of rabbit stompin' done properly; no siree, not a'tall.

For openers, one needs a contingent of preferably over-sized and tremendously clumsy buddies who don't mind walking three inches per day off their boot soles. Mixed in with the marathons will be several hundred well-aimed kicks, not to mention one or two highly amusing (to other hunters) episodes of tripping over unseen vines, limbs, and fallen fences.

The end result of this last is known in Southern Nimrod parlance as sprawling, and is largely self-explanatory. The

sprawling hunter will never wind up in any location other than the precise geometric center of the most devilish briar patch within three counties. This patch does yeoman duty in guaranteeing various mercurochrome, gauze, and peroxide-manufacturing companies huge annual profits.

Sprawling of this sort is almost always accompanied by a multitude of quaint local sayings dealing with the patch's appearance, location, and ancestry. It takes only slightly longer than the span of the last Ice Age to extricate oneself after the peformance, and it does slow the hunting process somewhat. As gun-totin' companions are rather intently watching this extrication process, they may notice a slight ripping sound or three as young briars decide to leave the nest and go out on their own at last.

The victim will reassure Mother Briar's household in the same soothing voice he uses to break up dog fights. Then he'll be on his way with a completely new outlook on life and (mostly) death, having a near-uncontrollable urge to kill something quickly.

But sprawling is only one minor part of stompin' for rabbits. As everyone who has spent any time at all chasing him down knows, Ol' Longears will take to his heels only until he gets to a favorite hideout. He will then hole up like that Saturday morning bad guy, Black Bart, who stays out of sight, too, until my boyhood hero, the King of the Cowboys—Roy Rogers—flushes him out.

Sprawling by the hunter provides a brief respite for the hunted, kind of like the one Bart always gets. To wit: even as the devilish outlaw is at last cornered, meanwhile, back at the ranch, Ol' Roy's low-IQ sidekick has been mistaken for a cattle rustler and is in the process of being lynched. Loyalty forces Roy to hustle Trigger out of Bart's neighborhood and all the way back to his goofy buddy's rescue. At that point, the process starts all over again: Bart will resume raiding, robbing, and riding down old ladies trying to cross the street until he is corraled after falling off his horse at the end of yet another wild chase. After all, it's hard to keep a grip on the reins when your sixgun's been shot out of your hand the last six Saturdays in a row!

The area where Bart and/or the rabbit went to ground is usually the thickest in the particular hemisphere in which the two reside. Like Roy, the hunter has no choice other than to try to kick his quarry out of hiding. Sometimes that happens, and we go on to our next exciting episode in rabbit stompin': gotimitis.

A hunter is stricken with gotimitis immediately upon taking a shot at something that very much resembles a hairy football moving at the speed of light. After all, the rabbit is going along with the fun, and just wants to make things a little more challenging. So, he stretches his legs.

The hare presents a brief glimpse of his hide to the man with the gun, who promptly bush-hogs an acre of countryside with a couple pounds of number six shot. As his companions call for results of the shot, it strikes. "Got 'im," the shooter chortles as he saunters to the spot where the rabbit is presumed to be stretched out like Bart following the final showdown.

Yep, you guessed it: noooo rabbit!

The hunter does, however, hear something that sounds very much like a giggling hare some thousand yards away. (Rabbit giggles, by the way, are not to be confused with the "Haw haw haw" of fellow hunters.)

Wearing his feelings, not to mention a few other items with sharp points, on his sleeve, our hero moves on to the next brush pile. The rabbit has left no forwarding address as he waltzed his way across the county, but the guy with the helpless gun is undaunted. Quicker than a gnat's hiccup, he's stomped out another one. The gun roars, gotimitis strikes, and rabbit giggles drown out the "haw haw haws." By now you get the picture.

At hunt's end, there is the final part of the trip, known as the account. This comes when someone, probably days later, asks the hunter to tell all about his outing. The reason it is days later is because the part of the world in which the actual hunt took place is just now returning to normal. Local volunteer fire departments have completed week-long livestock evacuations, coaxing cows, hogs, and sheep down from barn and tree tops at last. Large doses of liquid nerve relaxer have been mixed into watering troughs and coffee pots all over the county. It also takes a while for the rabbit population to recover from such a sweep through their domain. After all, your ribs would be sore from that much giggling, too.

But the hunter never mentions sprawling, gotimitis, or rabbit giggling during the course of the account. It is a glowing tribute to his consummate skill at shooting and the hunt in general. He can go on for hours about how accurate his shotgun is, and how he has no peer when it comes to pulling himself out of briars that would make an iron maiden look like a mattress commercial.

By the way, the account almost always ends with the by-now-unwilling recipient inquiring into the scrumptious taste of rabbit hams virtually breaststroking in thick, brown gravy. The hunter, though vague at first, finally mumbles something like, "Don't know; never tried it."

That sound strange to you?

14

THE BIG RABBIT RETURNS

T ravis Davis was holding court as the old pickup skidded and slid down the wet, red clay road, and he looked back occasionally to see if the truck behind us had disappeared, as into either of two very available and beckoning ditches.

"Deer ain't nothing but a big rabbit nohow," he asserted between juicy brown expectorations into a plastic cup. "You find a clearcut that's been planted over and you'll find rabbits when the trees are little. They hide the rabbits then; when they're up big enough to hide a deer, you'll find him there, too."

Far be it from me to argue. For one thing, I had found his assertion to be right on the mark. Secondly, Travis is only a little bit stronger than a mature bull buffalo, and the two are built along much the same lines. Nawsir, I ain't arguing.

The dogs in the back knew we were getting close as the Ford slowed to a crawl and swung into the field road. The impatient pack was raising vocal murder wanting out of the traveling box.

"Shut the nevermind up!" they were rudely instructed as the bunch of us crawled stiffly out into the first gray swirls of daylight. Coffee, black as a cutthroat's heart and stronger than new love, came smoking out of its battered plastic holder and into cups being proferred all around.

"Drink it black or do without." Almost everybody drinks; nobody complains.

Heavy coats feel good right now, but it won't be long until they become useless baggage, shed and hung high on tree limbs for later retrieval. The dogs are whining, with an occasional deep-voiced bawl from Ol' Doc thrown in to let us know we ain't being hospitable.

"W-w-well, are w-w-we going or not?" sixteen-year-old David Walden chatters in some semblance of a question. This is Travis's nephew. The boy don't drink coffee; if he did, he wouldn't stutter.

I don't tell him, of course, but I really like this kid. He's one of the rare ones these days who knows how to listen and learn without overly flapping his trap. As Daddy used to say, "You ain't learning nothing when you're talking."

Scatterguns are dragged out, always my favorite time. I'm gonna get rid of this Eskimo jacket and put on a vest, cause things'll heat up shortly. Count out the few high-brass fours that go into the left-hand pocket. A box of sixes, loosed, balances out the right. Swampers and cottontails, you know. Swampers don't deserve less than fours, because they can lead some mighty good beagle races, and should be taken as neatly and cleanly as possible . . . providing, of course, one ever gets a look at them.

"Turn 'em out."

Tee Turner flips a couple of latches and within seconds we're up to our ankles in steaming dog weewee. There's nothing to do but wait until the hounds are empty and satisfied, so we stand and shiver.

Peaches, being a she-male, has no such problem as do Doc and Little Man, so she has already taken off down the field road, running like her tail was afire.

"That's all right; we'll get that wildness out of her and she'll be plopped in the shade of the tailgate before the day's through," was roughly the thought running through my head as she suddenly opened up on an obviously red-hot trail. It is truly amazing what a beagle can do toward speeding up the loading process of a shotgun.

Travis and I took off one way, David the other. Tee perched on a spot at the approximate position where the rabbit got up.

We had that sucker surrounded!

A half hour later, I was beginning to wonder. Man, we were in the jungle. Webster ain't invented the word that will let you know what this place looked like. It was mostly a case of squat and scour the local terrain as far as the eye could see, which was quite a bit less than far. The dogs were looping, and there was no telling how much ahead of them their quarry was or where it was headed.

Somewhere along the way, Travis and I blundered into each other and pulled up for a breather. We could hear David forty yards away across a small creek and called to him to come on over for a parlay. About that time, the dogs turned.

"Coming back this way, Uncle Travis," came from across the water.

"Stand still," we informed him as one.

The dogs' high-pitched wails grew loud enough to break all the glass in a neighborhood . . . but we weren't in one. They were getting close, both to us and to whatever they were chasing.

When we first heard the crashing, Travis said he thought it was a deer. It was my personal opinion that the hounds were running a grizzly, and to that end I began looking for the nearest condominium-sized tree to shinny up. Meanwhile, on the other side of the creek . . .

David, as mentioned, is a young man, and he hasn't seen all that many deer up close and personal. That was about to change, and he will probably never again see one in the bloom of health this close again.

The buck, for that is indeed what it was, came zipping by within two feet of young Mr. Walden who, supercharged with adrenalin and puberty, could only squeak, "Deer, Uncle Travis, deer."

We're talking about a very nice whitetail within dental work distance of a kid with both hands full of shotgun, and never a shot was fired. Don't talk to me about whether it's kosher, much less legal, to plug a buck with sixes unless you've ever been in the path of a runaway whitetail. I have a sneaking suspicion that the both of us as sixteen-year-olds—and I had never even seen a deer in the wild at that age—well might have pounded that skeester had we had the chance and been in the proper terrified state of mind.

Maybe, after all, a deer ain't nothing but a big rabbit. Maybe there's a conspiracy, in which the big boys band together with the small ones to confound dogs and send hunters in search of ever-stronger doses of nerve-soothing snake oil. I can't give you the solution. But I can tell you that the next time we hunt that area, I'm takin' grenades.

15

THE FIRST TIME

There were rumors floating around back in the early days of my existence about those things called "deer" inhabiting woods up north, which area is defined as anything the other side of Atlanta or maybe stretching as far Arctic-ward as Chattanooga. That latter metropolis must have had a population of at least five hundred and was only a mile or so below the Canadian border as far as I was concerned at the time. It's nothing less than spectacular how many folks have moved in and how far south Chattanooga has sprawled since then!

After hearing one of these early tales, I quickly informed the gossipmonger that the information didn't bother me much a'tall, just as long as they didn't come down South messing around. After all, we didn't care much for interruptions in our squirrel and rabbit hunting, not to mention dove shoots and daily cold weather tests of bird dog talent.

"You don't understand!" the informant said as he gave a pretty impressive brogan stomp. Why he would get excited because I didn't understand was beyond me; that state of mind was surely nothing new.

"These deer are animals, just like all that stuff you're always dragging in. They're big ol' thangs that live and eat amongst the trees and fields."

"They live in the trees like squirrels?" My interest was suddenly and definitely piqued.

"No, you batbrain, they can't climb trees. I'm talking about how they live in the woods and come out into folks' fields to eat up their corn and such."

Well, that did it. He was obviously funnin' me, trying to con a poor old dumb country boy into believing there was a separate species of coon that couldn't climb. But I was too smart for that. After all, barbecued coon had been on the menu around our place for most of my days, and I knew they could climb anything this side of polished glass and get it done quick, too. Popping my overhaul galluses with both thumbs, I was in the process of salvaging a piece of my pride and walking away when, with an audible tinge of desperation, he said, "But people up there hunt these deer all the time; and eat 'em, too."

Bells went to clanging and lights started flashing, because two magic words had shown up in that one little old sentence. My head snapped back like a first-week Marine bumping into a five-star general. Although he was now sulling like a ticked-off possum because I hadn't believed him at first, my new instructor was quickly persuaded to elaborate.

"Tell me about how you hunt 'em and eat 'em and I won't tell your wife who I saw you skinnydippin' with down at the creek yesterday," I blatantly threatened.

Naturally, I now know absolutely everything there is to be learned about hunting and eating deer. However, most of it came from personal experience, because this was about the dumbest clod in our county.

Interestingly enough, not long after this conversation my Granddaddy brought home a couple of coolers packed with venison, part of it to be processed by the Human Gnawing Machine, otherwise known as Yours Truly.

One of my grandparents' grandest celebrations was their annual trip to "Flardy," otherwise known as the great state of Florida, where they had spent much of their early years. The red meat had been obtained on one of those jaunts. From what I understood at the time, this deer was rather under-educated when it came to the process of crossing highways, and became very suddenly acquainted with about forty thousand pounds of my folks' early-'60s Chrysler.

At trip's end the meat was hauled home, and on the night it was to be served up I remember that I was so excited about getting a taste that I passed up the first five minutes of the greatest TV show of all time: *Gunsmoke*.

Not that it took that long to eat; in fact, it took only about two seconds. The rest of the time was spent trying to rid my cavernous maw of the taste, which closely resembled that of a Pontiac radiator hose boiled in castor oil. It was the first and last Grandma ever cooked, and although it wasn't really the buck's fault, I've held a grudge against deer ever since and demonstrate that fact to them at each and every opportunity. But there has come, over the years, a recipe or two that dramatically changed my views on their edibility.

Plus, they are so very much fun to hunt. Take number one, for example . . .

THE OLD TENANT HOUSE HAD STOOD FOR MANY A YEAR BEFORE OUR hunting group took it over as a camphouse project. There was a heck of a lot of work to be done, and not a lot of time to do it, to get the place into shape. But we were all excited about it. As things stood, we had two months before opening day of deer season, and my first trip after an animal that I have come to respect and love like no other. There's just nothing like 'em.

There were four of us hunters, all but me having chased whitetails for several years. I know for a fact that two of the other three had never killed one. Although the fourth swears he had, it is common knowledge that he has sworn to a fifty-five-gallon-drum-full of other outright lies in his day. Despite their lack of success, oh, did they ever give me grief about what a greenhorn they were taking, and how lucky I was to be included in the group. Par for the course, I guess.

Those two months before opening morning, I had worked my buns off at learning every possible tip and trick from deer-hunting articles as far as picking a location, setting up a stand, checking what the weather was going to do, looking at the wind . . . you name it, I checked it.

That's why, on Wednesday before the season opened on Saturday, I finally decided to use the grand total of four nails and secure a single piece of plywood across a perfectly-forking pair of oak limbs fifteen feet off the ground. The stand was in a big tree located less than a hundred yards from a gravel-topped highway and well within sight of our camphouse and the home of the local judge!

Friday night, as my companions stood by the camphouse fireplace after a steak supper (that I had prepared!) and discussed where they would be hunting at daylight the next morning, the ribbing started all over again.

The location of my "stand" drew roars of laughter, as did the fact that I would be shooting my old sixteen-gauge automatic shotgun. The gun was infinitely better for deer hunting, in my opinion, than the other one I owned, which happened to be a .22 rifle. That the sixteen did not match up to their high-powered rifles was no great secret, but as one of my favorite big-screen characters once said in what has become my personal motto, "A man's got to know his limitations."

If I knew nothing else, I knew that shotgun. We had been on intimate terms with one another since a certain fateful birthday dove shoot. Besides, in those days I couldn't afford to purchase one of the cartridges they had pockets full of, much less the high-powered rifles themselves.

"Just put up with the guff and take your chances," I silently resolved, and continued munching on an absolutely exquisite slab of grilled cow.

Walking to the stand next morning, it struck me that this was very likely the coldest day in the history of the world. Nailed-down handholds leading up to the plywood itself were torturous to fingers rendered as stiff as an old horseshoe. But, all things considered and finally settling in, my hopes were high.

The tree was located at the apex of a triangle of twin fields and a hundred-acre measure of thick woods. To the right was corn; soybeans stretched to the left, and several white oaks like the one I was perched in were spread throughout the trees behind.

Corn provides both food and cover for deer; the acorns of the white oak are a staple when in season. Soybeans are delicacies both before and after there are any acorns to be found. As far as the nearby buildings and road, that had never seemed to bother any deer I ever read about, and so were dismissed.

Not so the truck that swung into the field, however. It stopped within fifty feet of my tree as my first deer-hunting dawn was at last breaking. The pickup was strange, but I immediately recognized the driver . . . which didn't do much for my mood . . . as he stumbled out. He was a "friend of a friend" and in truth had no business being where he was. I knew it as well as he did.

"Patience," they say, "is a virtue." I wouldn't know. It is true that one mellows with age but at that stage of my life, like a good guard dog, I'd just as soon bite first and check for invitations later. Since he had to walk close by, however, it was too good a chance to pass up. So I waited until the guy had pulled on his heavy coat, grabbed a gun, slammed the door, and walked under my personal pair of limbs in the deep gray of dawn before I exclaimed in something slightly more forceful than chitchat, "Get that truck out of here!"

He did, too, although for a while I thought I was going to have to crawl down and jump-start his heart and, following his recovery, convince the lad that he really didn't want me down from the tree in the first place. I had been accused before of being young, among other things, but seldom of being small.

It's a sad state of affairs to sit upon one's very first deer stand and realize that even though you have worked as hard as humanly possible to keep things quiet, only slightly more noise than twin typhoons would make has recently occured in the vicinity. The minutes slipped past and the wild world began re-awakening and re-emerging following the exit of the noisy pickup and its noxious driver. Still, there remained a niggling of doubt gnawing at all the high expectations.

Maybe that's what made it so special when, after thirty minutes had wormed their way by, a gorgeous eight-pointer came loafing out of the corner of the corn, took an abrupt left and walked ten feet out in front and fifteen feet down from where I sat.

It was deathly still as each of the buck's steps spoke to my heightened senses. The two of us were alone in the world. Spray frothed lightly from his nostrils with each frozen breath, even as I tried to hide my own. Muscles rippled under his tawny hide; his head was up and ever aware, but not overly so.

Senses matched senses, mine and his. I recall being deathly afraid that my heart would leap onto his back and spook him, or maybe that the safety snicking off would send him humping it into the next area code.

Slower than you'll ever know unless you've been there, the old Winchester tucked itself gently into its home away from home on my shoulder. I could actually hear the buck breathe as he moved, each hoof as it crunched into the frozen ground. But he was caught completely unawares, despite being within a handful of steps from where the truck driver had been mere minutes before. His nose failed him, as did his ears when the safety changed positions.

A shattering roar split the silence and sent number one buckshot ripping into the buck's neck from above, almost driving him into the ground. His nose was the first thing to hit the ice, and his ribs bounced down next. There was a single kick of the huge hind legs, instantly bringing another trigger pull for insurance.

Still.

All is silent. I locked in on him, shoving a couple more rounds of buck in the sixteen's maw. If he got up, I knew I could need at least one more shot, so the automatic digested its loads quickly. After sitting for so long and so cold, I was now standing upright on a piece of plywood that was not guaranteed to balance my act in the most perfect state of mind, much less my present one. The deer was directly below, his left rear leg weaving ever-smaller circles.

Breath came hard. The coat was suddenly very hot, but there was no way to take it off with finger on trigger and eyes glued to bead. With a final drop of one of the legs that had propelled him through so much, he was gone.

I had killed my first whitetail buck.

16

AFTERMATH

My first deer had been dressed, or more fittingly "undressed." Back at the camphouse the rifle-toters were dragging in. They had seen, shot at, and killed a total of zero, zilch, approximately NO bucks, and the boys were grumbling.

Ain't this terrible?

"What y'all goin'ta eat boys?"

"Sounds like a hongry night to me."

"Grumbling bellies gonna keep me awake all night long."

There were venison steaks, about as fresh as steak could get, sizzling on the grill outside. They had been sliced thin, marinated in Worcestershire sauce and garlic salt for twenty minutes, then slapped on hot coals. I could tell by the way my fellow hunters' top lips curled up around their noses that they appreciated the smell.

Finally, I queried, "Would y'all really like a piece of that meat even after it's been blasted by an old shotgun?"

Don't believe I'll repeat the replies.

We ate like starving wolves, all of us. Next morning, there were more deer to hunt, and I really and truly hoped someone else would score. Someone, in a manner of speaking, did.

THERE WAS A GOOD-SIZED PASTURE, WHICH HAD FORMERLY BELONGED TO cows currently gracing grocery store meat counters, directly behind the camphouse. Since we as yet had no indoor plumbing, the renowned Half-Moon House, otherwise known as the Reading Room, was positioned at the fence separating the pasture and our back yard. The camphouse's original roofing tin, stripped off in favor of something that would keep us slightly drier, had been loosely piled by that same fence by Buddy, caretaker of the farmland we hunted.

Buddy was about as old as dirt, only slightly younger than rocks and had lived on the place forever. He was getting too ornery and arthritic to do much of anything except look after basics and occasionally take a tractor ride and spot all the feeding whitetails . . . the more to tell us about later, my dear.

By the way, if you're unfamiliar with hunting in farming territory, be advised that our deer pay about as much attention to tractors as New York City drivers pay to other New York City drivers.

We all went out stepping high that second dawn, although I must admit experiencing a modicum of letdown. My status as a deer hunter had been elevated greatly within the past twenty-four hours, with not a little envy involved. It was now my intent to help a friend drag in something.

About two hours after crunching ice and frozen ground to reach my perch, I could see the brand-new tin of the camphouse roof gleaming invitingly in a brilliant morning sun. Deciding that 120 minutes were long enough, and not a little apprehensive about killing another deer since I had heard no other guns going off, I climbed down and took off to the warmth of the camphouse fire.

On the trip back, my excuse for a mind was vacationing somewhere among bikinis and island breezes as I walked down an iced-over roadside. Turning carefree at last into the camphouse lane, I witnessed a sight that will live in infamy within the cobwebs of my brain: that old caretaker barreling as fast as he could move . . . which was roughly twelve times quicker than I ever suspected . . . across the front threshold, leaving the screen door flapping on its hinges. That scene in itself was enough to draw my undivided attention, but the fact that he was tightly clutching a battered Mossberg pump gun definitely perked my ears up . . . even as the rest of me hit the grass.

"Youseethatdangdeerhenearlyscairtmetodeath," or something along those lines, came out of his gaping gums in one jumbled word.

"Buddy. Hey, Buddy," was all I could screech, fully believing my days were too soon at an end, and praying that he could see that I wasn't whatever was chasing him.

Eventually, as I slunk into the highest stuff available and none of it high enough, he calmed down and quarter-miled over to explain that a certain deer had in fact nearly scared him to death seconds before he pulled the same stunt on me.

It seems that while we who hunt went one way, all the deer came the other, including the misguided buck that took a year or two off Buddy's life. The old man had been er, uh, reading his morning paper in a certain facility with a half-moon on the door when the small mountain of old tin around him noisily came to life.

The big whitetail, spooked by somebody or other, had jumped the fence, hit the iced-over tin with all four feet, fallen heavily, then thrashed around on the slick stuff attempting to get up . . . while Buddy did the same, his bodily functions having been greatly accelerated. The old man came blowing out of his confined spaces just as his counterpart did, one keeping perfect stride with the other as they headed for the house.

One went past the house, one went in the house, and as the second party was emerging from the house too late,

shotgun in hand, I showed up, somehow having completely missed seeing the deer.

Story of my life.

THAT WAS SOME PLACE, THAT OLD HOUSE, BUT NOT NEARLY AS INTERESTING as the surrounding land. We had deer, friends, trust me. We had more deer than the bunch of us is likely to see again in a long while. None of them set the tone for the future of my whitetail hunting as did the last one I killed on the premises. But there were lessons to be learned before then.

That shotgun did its job as well as could be expected of any scattergun in the deer woods, but I was young, poor, and ignorant at the time. I have been older, poorer, and seemingly much more ignorant since, but I well remember the day I made the decision to change to a weapon with higher velocity.

Fifty yards behind the spot where my first deer fell was a second stand, overlooking a very narrow—maybe sixty yards wide—bean field corner. In late afternoon, deer were prone to hold hoedowns, raffles, and high-society socials in the beans, swapping small talk and nibbling on high-protein delicacies compliments of our farm hands and pocketbooks.

After killing that first buck, I came to the asinine decision that henceforth I was a trophy hunter, and nothing smaller than eight points would I send chunks of lead toward. After passing up a pile of extremely legal does and juvenile bucks, the season came very suddenly to its finale.

It was upon that backup stand, shotgun in hand on the last morning of the season, that I saw the largest whitetail buck then in existence. He was two hundred yards away, walking across a wide-open, now-harvested field. His head, bobbing up and down uncomfortably under the weight of an upside-down rocking chair, never turned toward me. Mine never turned away from him. That deer, at ten of the A.M. on a diamond-bright morning, was as nonchalant as an animal can get. The sight of him plodding through that field haunts me still.

"I will have," I resolved as he finally disappeared totally outside my gun's range, "a rifle. And hang the cost."

Very soon after, I acquired a Remington automatic, .30-06 in caliber. Whitetail herds from Flardy to Canada have never forgiven me.

By the way, while we're on the subject of that rifle, let me put in at least my two cents worth solely from a satisfied gunowner's standpoint. Say what you will about the automatic rifle and its accuracy as compared to the bolt-action. I am an outdoors writer; however, I certainly lay no claim to being a ballistics expert. But it is with a silent chuckle and maybe a side-to-side sweep of the noggin that I listen to so-called experts scoff at the one action and laud the other. I know only what my rifle has done for over twenty years . . . and will do today. For instance . . .

My second deer, a doe, was killed with this gun and shot at a distance I would never have believed possible. Oh yes, at the time I, too, had faith in what others had written and vowed, namely that the auto was useless beyond a couple hundred yards. But after running quite a few practice rounds through the ought-six, I was seriously questioning their veracity. One frigid morning, I found out just what that 742 could do . . .

As my old truck swung into the highway just after six a.m., I spotted the doe. I was headed to work, and dawn was slashing gory streaks through a slate-gray morning. The big female was dining on stolen grapes, or more accurately stolen soybeans, across the field in front of my home. Hmmmm . . .

She was not in the least impressed with me, although I was pretty taken. My thoughts raced. "Wonder how stupid she is? Will she wait until I pull back in, grab the new gun, come back, load up, and get off a shot?"

Very, yes, yes, yes, yes, and yes.

That was one dumb deer. Realizing full well that my situation was "I owe, I owe, so off to work I go," and that there was no time for dilly-dallying around chasing punctured whitetails,

I decided to shoot for the very small target of her head.

What the heck? If I miss, she runs; if I don't, she won't. A body shot would probably require a chase, however brief, and a follow-up shot, and the time factor . . . not to mention my crabby old boss . . . wouldn't allow that.

She watched all the while like Saturday morning at the westerns as the gun was nestled onto barbed wire and snugged to a post. Mentally factoring in distance and putting the 4X crosshairs just over the tip of an ear, I squeezed off.

I lost sight of her in the recoil, and as the scope swept back over the vicinity, only soybeans were visible. But I could pretty much call that shot. There was no way she had run. Covering the distance carefully, senses tuned in for any threat of flight, I walked up on her as dead as a hammer. The 150-grain bullet had gone in just below the ear. She never even heard the gun go off.

After she was dropped off at the farm cooler to be hung until I could get her unzipped, I drove . . . or floated . . . on to the job. After getting the morning crew started, I came right back with a co-worker and a hundred-foot steel tape. Swinging the tape back and forth as we went, we ticked off three hundred and thirty yards . . . exactly . . . from fence post to puddle of blood. Not bad shooting for an automatic rifle, or any other type, regardless of who's behind it.

That is longer than I will shoot, at most whitetails at least, under almost any circumstances. Send me a rocking-chair buck across a harvested field again and I might just touch it off at a thousand yards, however.

Seriously, do not simply read what other folks write and decide what a gun will or will not do. Find out for yourself. Like snowflakes, no two people are alike when it comes to shooting a firearm. The guns themselves and how they fit you also vary greatly. Therefore, sight in your own and shoot it, by gum, until you are certain-sure where every bullet will wind up. From there, shoot it some more, and often.

17

ONE BRIGHT BUCK

Somewhere along the line, after hours, days, weeks, months, and years of hard work, study, failures, and some successes . . . those basic tools of learning . . . I came to be, in my humble opinion, a pretty fair deer hunter. Then, too, I've met some pretty stupid deer, which have a chapter or two all their own down the line.

Conversely, there were others that obviously had a higher IQ than mine, which in itself admittedly is no great feat. But there was one buck in particular, a nine-pointer, that held regular classes for my personal benefit. This was one smart deer, hear? He also set the stage for an episode that I will cherish until my final breath is drawn. The morning it happened came very close to providing that opportunity, because I almost laughed myself to death. It was like this . . .

IT IS MONDAY MORNING, A SULTRY DAY BREAKING WITH THE WHINE OF Middle Georgia's own licensed brand of killer mosquitos. Opening day of whitetail season is five sunrises hence. Hearty bands of nimbus clouds are scudding behind each other up top, promising relief from the heat and crunching leaves.

If I've figured right over the past four days, the buck should be working up the sandy bottom this morning. Yesterday, he came through the irrigation ditch, and he has been alternating between the two each morning on his way to the soybean field. Camera ready, I sit and wait.

Ten minutes pass, and several pints of blood are lost, before I know he's coming. It crosses my mind that I know a mosquito is tough when the opening of his switchblade knife can be heard just before he slices through the fabric of trouser legs. But the crunch of hooves on leaves erases any thought of swatting. Here he comes, right on schedule.

Tuesday morning dawns cooler. It is Ditch Day, and I am in position among the limbs of a huge fallen oak, a perfect natural blind if ever there was one. He should come this way today, passing by the Nikon like a starving model. The blood-suckers aren't so bad today. Hope things will continue this way.

Wednesday, and he travels the sand route. The paths are about a hundred yards apart, and he has not deviated for a week now. Let him pass and then I'll pull out; don't want too much human scent in the woods this time of year. Saturday morning, for sure, he'll pass by the fallen oak.

The shot won't be more than twenty yards, if that far, so for that reason alone, I decided to carry the deadliest short-range weapon on earth: the shotgun. The .30-06 was left hanging, and probably pouting, on the wall. It had done everything asked of it the past season, but there was pretty thick cover this time of year, and the shotgun's buckshot would do a better job of penetrating anything I had to shoot through. Besides, that shotgun seemed like an extension of my right arm, handling itself automatically in split-second situations. Yeah, I had best take it along.

So now you know all the reasoning behind my idiotic decision.

In case you haven't figured out yet which path the big whitetail used on opening morning, try one more time. As I sat comfortably, supremely confident and perfectly camouflaged among the hardwood, there came a slight sound from a hundred yards behind. Easing around and knowing what I'd see before I saw it, I spotted the buck. He didn't know I was within a hundred miles, and I might just as well have been that far away.

I knew better than to shoot. Buckshot is just not reliable enough at that distance, especially in a sixteen-gauge, and this was a very nice trophy. Later, long after he had moved out of the area, I made a singularly spectacular trip back to the truck, face as red as a beet, stomping everything within reach and vowing to purchase an automatic butt-kicking machine to hook myself up to at the earliest opportunity. There ain't a self-respecting nurse on the planet who wouldn't have wanted a shot at my bulging veins that morning. I'm just glad it was too cool for the mosquitos or I may not have lived to write this.

Yessir, the good ol' ought-six, which would have allowed me to pick which hair on his hide I wanted to shoot at, had its revenge for being left hanging.

For three trips over the next two weeks, no nine-pointer was to be found. None of the four of us on the place had taken him . . . or anything else, for that matter . . . and I was beginning to wonder about that plague on the face of the earth: poachers. Surely the hunting gods wouldn't allow as magnificent an animal as this to be jacklighted and dragged off to have his rack and hams hacked out, then dumped in a ditch somewhere.

Believe me when I say that on the fourth morning there were no mosquitos to be seen. It was as cold as the proverbial welldigger's extremities as I settled into the now nearly-leafless limbs of that oak tree, Remington in hand. This was it. I felt it. Just me and that buck, alone in the brittle blackness. It was destined.

And then a truck door slammed.

Two hundred yards away, one of my hunting partners had driven in from the other side of my stretch of woods. The terrain was such that he would be facing one bean field while I faced the other, back-to-back. But day would be breaking pretty soon, and he needed to hurry in and settle down. One very pertinent piece of information that I was not aware of was that, only the day before, he had purchased a new-fangled climbing stand.

No big deal, right?

Consider, though, that this was back in the days when the climbing tree stand was in its infancy. The very first models came equipped with a single, very small platform and a wide-V blade that unscrewed to wrap around a tree, cut into it under the hunter's weight, then up, ostensibly, he went. For you non-hunters, let me further explain that in the beginning, we strapped our feet onto the platform, hugged the tree, kicked the blade away, then pulled ourselves up. Drawing the feet and seat up, we then stomped down hard to make the blade bite on the back side of the tree.

All this required quite a bit of upper-body strength and fairly good balance. Beer bellies, such as my partner was a proud possessor of, helped not at all. Finally, while this was done a little at a time and . . . believe me . . . as carefully as possible, the process made only a tad more noise than World War Twice.

Seething helplessly by, knowing that every deer within a mile was acutely aware of what was going on, I was basically basting in my own temperamental juices when some very interesting sounds suddenly erupted from the direction of my companion. Initially, it sounded like someone scraping scales off a gigantic bass. Next came a wild bellow very closely resembling, "OH, SHEILA."

That was followed by brisk sliding sounds accompanied by intermittent "thunks" as the blade did its best to bite back into the tree on occasion and thus slow the downward progression of hunter and stand. The guy kept hollerin' for his sweetheart

all the way to the ground, although the closer he got the higher-pitched his voice became. Also, it picked up a certain bluegrass twang, but that was probably from all the bark up his nose. I don't know if Sheila ever heard him, but it was for sure that I, and one other main character in this act, did.

With just enough light to make him out, that nine-pointer came ballin' the jack by me, heading out like he was going to Egypt on a tight schedule. From my knees . . . honestly . . . and with tears of laughter streaming down my face, I gave that big rascal 150 grains of eternal happiness just behind the eyelashes. That didn't do much for his complexion, and so his head is not resting over my fireplace at this moment. Nonetheless, he will always hold a special place in my heart, because he was one animal that stood rack and shoulders above most members of a species that is number one in my heart and the hearts of hunters all across the Great Forty-eight.

And the other hunter with the climbing stand? Although he vowed that he was in only slightly better shape than your average helicopter crash victim, he was walking and talking. He was also oozing rather profusely from a series of nasty abrasions. And his mood closely resembled that of a tiger who's just had a large steak snatched away from his choppers. Upon eyeballing my buck, he was in an even worse mood, envy having wormed its evil way into his heart.

But he was, and remains, a basically good old soul, and was finally able to laugh at himself. Thus, I escaped his wrath and the entire episode unscathed . . . even if he and my smart-but-spooked nine-pointer did not.

18

SHOTGUNS VS. RIFLES

How much do you know about your gun? Come on, be honest. Nobody but me and (mostly) you will ever know. Hey, the only way you're ever going to learn anything is to stumble onto it, be told, read, or ask. Ever thought about it?

After a couple of the aforementioned fiascos with Odocoileus virginianus, in which I played mostly the role of anus, I decided to come to a decision about guns, once and for all. The wallhanger strutting through the harvested field provided the initial thought. Then came the episode of the big nine-pointer that tipped the scales in favor of the rifle over the shotgun. And then? Well, here came the kicker . . .

HAVING MAPPED OUT A HOLIDAY WEEKEND OF VACATION HUNTING, I WAS overjoyed to hear the weatherman's prediction of cold, dry days ahead. You may imagine, if you have a slightly demented personality, my wishes for the future of that forecaster as I sat huddled under dripping branches, feeling rather like a bag of lumpy oatmeal, icy water drizzling relentlessly down.

About an hour in the tree was all it took to reach the bounds of bearability. Fed and watered up, down I came. That was an adventure in itself which does not bear repeating here. I will say that a boot heel slipped on a wet limb, touching off a performance that closely resembled an overzealous octopus skidding down a pine.

Reaching terra firma with quite a thud but at least still mobile, I decided to still-hunt, or slip-hunt as it is commonly and more accurately known. I slogged off through the near-impenetrable countryside, secure in the knowledge that there was a nearby logging road which would provide access to both navigation and penetration.

Looking on the bright side, at least things weren't as noisy underfoot, although they were quite a bit damper. Thinking back on it now, I guess it was attempting to find that bright side which was to blame for my sudden and greatly-accelerated trip down an as yet unknown but up-and-coming mountain.

When one has a one-track mind and is walking a wet track, his mind should be down around his boot bottoms. Not noticing the especially slick spot thereunder is understand-able, because horizontal shapes . . . such as a deer's belly or back . . . were the main items my radar-like baby blues were scanning to discern. There was no use in looking for a whole deer as such, because things were just too thick.

But if I didn't spot the slick spot, it definitely didn't miss me. One moment I was slip-hunting, the next simply slipping, along with a lot of sliding.

As I skidded ever downward through the muck . . . and not ungracefully, I might add . . . I was pleasantly surprised to glance up and spy a whitetail doe watching me with a look of admiration and awe. The fact that this was an either-sex day and she was as legal as keno in Tahoe didn't seem to dawn on her until we were a couple of car lengths apart. Or maybe she had come to the realization that no one could get off a shot from an upside-down position while sliding at the speed of sound. At any rate, I finally righted myself and threw up the rifle, only to see her bound off. Tauntingly, she stopped fifty feet or so away, a sapling screen between me and the couple pieces of deer that I could make out.

A shot would hit her, no doubt, but where? Would it put her down? How much deflection would there be? Gut shot? No, thanks. The safety was never even thumbed off, and she eventually melted off into the dripping trees. If only I had my shotgun . . .

And here we go again. A veritable Pandora's box of argument touched itself off. Hang it all, let's just find out what we need to know about scatterguns.

Twelve gauge, sixteen gauge, twenty gauge, what's the difference? A piled-up heap, especially when it comes to deer hunting. "Gauge" of a shotgun . . . and most hunters probably don't know this even if they won't admit it . . . is determined by the number of lead balls that would perfectly fit the gun's bore and make up a pound.

For instance, a round lead ball that would drop snugly down the barrel of a twelve-gauge shotgun would weigh one-twelfth of a pound, and a dozen of them would total sixteen ounces, or seven thousand grains. A sixteen-gauge would require sixteen balls that collectively weigh a pound . . . something very closely resembling an ounce apiece . . . and so on.

There is an exception to every rule, and in the case of shotguns it is the .410 (with a decimal point). This is not a gauge at all, but the actual measurement in inches of the diameter of the bore itself.

Now that we know a little more about the gun itself, let's go on to its projectiles, such as rifled slugs and buckshot. Collectively, they make up probably the most misunderstood pieces of lead on this or any other continent.

Slugs, usually shaped like missiles with either pointed or round noses, are generally believed to be accurate and deadly at a hundred yards or better. If you ever kill a whitetail a hundred yards away with a rifled slug, please fall immediately to your knees in a fanatical and heavenly show of thanks, because you have just witnessed a miracle. At very close range, let's say up to sixty yards out, the rifled slug in the right gun and properly applied is about as effective as the offering of the Enola Gay (no relation) on Hiroshima. Let's consider a few more pertinent numbers.

A twelve-gauge slug weighs 415 grains. Compare that with the highly-touted knockdown power of the big blunt-nosed 220-grain .30-06 bullet and you begin to get the picture. (And that 220-grain is about as poor a choice as you will ever make for the whitetail; it's too bulky and tends to zip through without the all-important expansion of a 150-grain or thereabouts.) A sixteen-gauge slug tips the scales at 350 grains, still very adequate; the twenty-gauge weighs in at 282, and is questionable at any but the closest of ranges, such as when a twelve-pointer trips over your bootlaces.

The .410 slug is a 93-grain midget that is in roughly the same class as trying to kill a buck with a square-edged gravedigger's shovel: it can be done, but ain't likely to happen soon.

As far as range, let's look only at the twelve-gauge, and you can draw your own conclusions. At the muzzle, you have a 415-grain projectile traveling at 1,600 feet per second and delivering 2,480 foot-pounds of energy for knockdown power. One hundred yards away, that same 415 grains is moving at 960 feet per second and its energy has decreased a whopping 1,585 foot-pounds to a mere 960.

Now, class. What is it doing during all that slowing down? Remember your science lessons and the law of gravity? Thaaaaat's right, it's dropping like a rock. Now, where did you aim?

After sifting through all this, I hope you shotgun hunters will make the decision to put together a package of a twelve-gauge, preferably pump or automatic in case a second or third shot is needed, and stoke it with number one buckshot backed up by a pair of rifled slugs. The reasoning behind number one buck over the hallowed double-ought is simply that because of the shape and size of the pellets, many more No. 1s than double-oughts fit into a hull, providing by far more knockdown power.

In spite of any and all figures, I would absolutely refuse to shoot at a deer over fifty yards away, but that is purely personal preference. As far as that goes, I'd use a rifle, but that, too, is an idiosyncrasy put into place through equal measures of hard work and hard luck. The shotgun does have its advantages, quickness and ease of handling chief among them. Outfitted and used correctly, it can be a very effective weapon. Just make sure you know its strengths and limitations, as well as yours. Now, grab your weapon of choice and let's go hunting.

19

THE HIGHLY INTELLIGENT WHITETAIL

T he old man had been a true-loving turkey hunter for more decades than he cared to mention, and we young bloods were hanging on his every word. We had been discussing the relative merits of whitetail IQ versus turkey IQ when he joined in.

"Most people have heard that the gobbler is just about the smartest, wiliest creature on earth," the aging gent led off, "and to kill one, a hunter has to have the patience of Job and the wisdom of Solomon. But through my years of chasin' 'em, I've found that a turkey is about the stupidest thing in the woods. That's why they're so hard to figure out. After all, if they don't know which direction they're going in next, how can a hunter hope to head 'em off? Deers is probably that same way."

I'll have to take his word for it about the turkey, having never taken up the vice of hunting them. But I've shifted gears chasing "deers" many a time, and have found that whitetails just ain't stupid.

Well, most of 'em anyway. Opening-day deer are usually the lowest on the intelligence quotient scale, and there was one in particular . . .

It started as a low and distant rumble, droning ever closer as the misty daylight began to unfold. It reminded one of the dreaded roar of World War II's B-52 bomber squadrons. As I looked up, eyeballs still complaining from leaving home without coffee, I saw that the incoming group was more like a gaggle of bomber-protecting aircraft, nimble and deadly.

The first member peeled off and spiraled down directly onto my left wrist, battling his way through the camouflage netting of my gloves and piercing the skin like a whetstoned rapier. Barely stifling a howl, I splattered his blood . . . actually, I guess it was my blood . . . all over my lower arm. Then I remembered that I was deer hunting, and one of the prime requisites was to sit still.

As the second mosquito swooped in for a landing on my right thumb, which was gently cradling the rifle's pistol grip and otherwise minding its own business, I began swatting in earnest, deer be hanged. Shooting one of the attackers was strongly considered, but with only a .30-06, I felt seriously undergunned. It was for sure that I didn't want to wound one and have him turn on me in earnest.

Besides, I only carried ten bullets. That would be enough for a buck or two, or maybe ten, but I didn't want to chance them on these economy-sized bloodsuckers. Figuring submission was indeed the better part of valor, it was hunch up and take it, brushing one away now and then . . . very gently so as not to make any of them angry. Mercifully, the assault ended shortly after first light, and although I was about a quart low on blood, I did pull through.

So this is opening morning of deer season, huh? I was in a mood to propose opening an unlimited season on mosquitos, but then who'd be brave enough to shoot at one? If you've ever seen the movie *The Fly*, picture a mosquito on a comparable scale and you'll know what I was up against. If that attack was survived, nothing was going to make me leave the stand until a buck passed by or, preferably, passed on.

About two hours later, with booming going on all around from every living hunter's gun but mine, both legs were asleep and both butt cheeks paralyzed. With the rain now falling steadily down, I was beginning to have a change of heart as I sat on the ground under the overhanging limbs of a small oak.

Why the ground, you ask?

For starters, I do not like high places. In fact, I hate high places; anything over six feet, two inches is too high for me, and I sometimes walk in a stoop just so I won't be up that far. Also, there was no suitable spot on the edge of the field to place a ladder stand, and we do not build pine-tree condominiums on property belonging to folks nice enough to let us hunt there, do we?

Don't even mention climbing stands. Remember that nine-point episode? Well, I came down a slick oak the fast way one time too many myself, and the finally-healed hide on my chest and arms has never allowed me to live it down. Anyhow, I've killed more deer hunting from ground level than swaying among limbs and leaves. Me precious bod feels a wee bit more comfortable about bullet placement when its jangling nerves aren't screeching, "You're gonna fall, fool! Get down!"

Along the middle of the morning, golden leaves above the two big scrapes the buck had recently made began shining like new pennies. The rain had let up and sunshine was beginning to break through at last. Adrenalin surged, and the grip on the ought-six tightened. This is it: everything wearing deer hair just stood up and began to move, and he should be easing out of those hardwoods any minute now.

Didn't happen that way. Faking me out completely, the deer evidently had been bedding out in the middle of the head-high coffeeweed and other aggravating growth. I caught a glimpse of movement out of the corner of an eye, and instantly focused on a slow-moving rack literally glowing in the sun. He was easing toward those scrapes to mix up a little more whitetail-recipe Indian love call.

Great. Lovely. He's walking directly away. So what do we do now, Dan'l?

It strikes me as rather unsporting to plug him in the hiney. Oh sure, he's not going to appreciate it from either end, but a 150-grain enema, the old Alabama Brain Shot, is just not the way to start off a season. And think of the venison it will ruin.

Knowing that deer by nature are curious animals, and this early in the season unlikely to be overly spooky, I decided to turn him around by getting his attention. Not being a proud owner of a grunt call (a what?) back in those days, I did my best German shepherd imitation. Brother, that did it! That seven-pointer pulled up like he had been reined in, then craned his neck around to check things out.

He never knew what hit him. He was a pretty good-sized deer, too. In fact, by the time I dragged him to the truck and loaded him up, by my lonesome, I figured he'd dress out around a thousand pounds.

THIS NEXT ONE COMES DIRECTLY FROM THE RIPLEY'S UNCOORDINATED Bucks Division, and you can believe it or not. It is a once-and-only occurence . . . or at least I hope so.

I was hunting with a buddy, on (low) ladder stands about five hundred yards apart. We were trying to improve our chances by going out on a doe day. Along about 4:30 that afternoon, I heard Ed shoot, and there immediately followed a noise like Godzilla running through oak leaves while wearing rubber knee boots. It was a yearling six-pointer, moving like he had just hunkered down on hot coals, coming toward me from the direction of my partner.

Just as I picked him up in the open sights, not being able to get the scope's crosshairs on such a bobbing target, the fool ran headfirst into a ten-inch-thick sweet gum tree . . . which didn't budge a bit. We are talking about a CO-llision. He fell like a fur-bearing boulder, and I recall mentally congratulating

Ed for taking a nice little buckaroo, even if it wasn't an instant kill.

Unloading the rifle, I climbed down from the stand, automatically popped the clip back in . . . thank goodness . . . and walked on over to check him out. The bullet that had been in my rifle's barrel was now resting comfortably in some pocket or other. We were about thirty feet apart when the buck kicked himself to his knees and looked around to see if pieces of the sky were still falling. I don't know which of us was the most dumbfounded!

But I do know who acted first.

Grabbing the ejector on the Remington and slamming a round home, I popped him a quick one in the chops and he went down again, this time to stay. A few minutes later, when Ed walked up, I was still looking for the hole his shot had made.

As I told him the story and asked where he had aimed, he replied, "At the doe's head. I didn't want to have to follow up a heart shot and chase her into that creek bottom. She was about a hundred yards away, in the edge of the rough around the bean field. I missed her clean, and she didn't wait around to try her luck a second time. By the way, right now is the first time I've ever laid eyes on that buck . . ."

ONE OF MY FAVORITE FOLKS IN THIS GALAXY GOES BY THE NAME OF JOHNNY David Fountain. At the time he and I began our traipsing around together, Ol' John was a fireman by trade, a most dangerous way of making a living that does have its rewards. Chief among these is the work schedule: twenty-four hours on duty followed by forty-eight off.

Can you imagine having two out of every three days to hunt and fish, while still drawing a paycheck? Besides having a near-perfect occupation except, of course, for the twin specters of tragedy and death that ride the shoulders of firemen everywhere, Johnny also staked claim to some property on which roams a herd of the absolutely stupidest whitetail deer you could ever imagine. The two of us got into the deer hunting business together from the start, and I well remember the first one he ever dragged out of the woods. I wasn't with him for the shooting part, getting called in later to help with the dirty work. But with no more brains than this deer had, it needed to have been taken out of the herd . . .

JOHNNY'S ROUGH-LOOKING—ON THE OUTSIDE—'65 FORD PICKUP bounced its way down the field road, rattling and rumbling, the vitamin-enriched big-block engine purring through its headers like a well-fed cat. For you youngbloods, '65s were made of iron and steel, not plastic and paper, and were not imported. Therefore, they make a little extra but excusable racket. There are thousands of them still on the road, all functional, few fancy.

As soon as the black truck had reached a suitable put-in point for hunting, Johnny shut things down. He stepped out with a creak of door and began readying his pockets for a morning of communing with nature and her inhabitants, at least one of which would hopefully be heavy and well-racked. He pulled out the rifle, a wicked little .243, and stoked it full.

"Slam," went the truck door. Ready? Heck no, there's the butt cushion.

Creak. Retrieve. Slam.

Got everything now? Nope, forgot the fox pee cover scent.

Creak. Retrieve. Slam.

Okay, let's step over the fence.

"Whoa up there, mule," he thinks to himself as a sound almost slaps him cross-eyed. "What was that noise?"

There really was no question, because a squirrel may sound like a deer, a bird may sound like a deer, a chipmunk may sound like a deer, but a deer sounds exactly like a deer, and when several are involved there's no mistake at all.

So here Ol' John is, straddling a barbed-wire fence with the top strand held down by his left hand and a rifle in his right.

Three does happen to be staring him in the face from forty steps away, and they have just taken a few steps of their own.

"Did I not very recently make some noise truck-side so as to give y'all fair warning?" Johnny muses. "Should you gals not now be nearing western Wyoming at a gallop, if only you had a brain between you?" But they're not mind readers. And besides, Johnny's mind has just now shifted gears. Uh-oh. Something's behind them, and it is neither small nor bareheaded; maybe that's what's holding their interest.

It is a compelling scenario: rifle over shoulder, hand holding down barbed wire, whitetails all in "go" position. If the barbed wire is loosed, Johnny may well and suddenly become a soprano. The buck's head moves, showing off a high wide rack, and suddenly that wire isn't so sharp after all. The hunter's mind is filled with antlers and the other male's mind is evidently on something else, such as producing dem little deer chilrens, for instance. The she-males, annoyed at both of them for lack of initiative, pack their bags for a day of shopping at the mall and move off. As slowly and gently as is humanly possible, the strand of wire is loosed.

"BOOOOOOMMMM."

You little ladies hurry on your way now. The boy may not have been much of a deer hunter at the time, but he was a heckuva shot with a long gun. In fact, Johnny Fountain is just about the best rifle shot I know, and I know a few. And what the .243 did to that erstwhile man about town is not a matter for public perusal. I know, because I happened to be the one called in to perform the autopsy.

"Hello."

"I got one and I don't know what to do with it."

"Bullnevermind."

But I could tell he wasn't lying. This was actually his first deer, about as macho a nine-pointer as I've seen, and even over the phone it was evident that the now-hooked hunter's head was still in the clouds. We unzipped the buck together, step by step back at my place, but how he ever got that extremely large piece of meat back across that fence and singlehandedly onto the '65 remains a wonder.

Maybe adrenalin has something to do with it. Maybe you get fired up when you kill a big buck. And maybe, just maybe, this is what man as a predator, even after all these thousands of years of alleged evolution have added such soft underbellies to the lot of us, is supposed to feel.

Think so?

20

How Dumb Can They Get?

Somewhere down the line in establishing Johnny Fountain's deer herd, there must have been a grand old sire of a mossyhorns with all the smarts of a load of hay. He passed these genes to his progeny, whose collective evolutionary educations built on that wit and wisdom to the point that they are now almost as bright as creosoted fence posts. In balloting for Stupid Deer of the Year awards a couple of moons past, the vote was so close that we just couldn't decide, and so dual honors were handed out. Fountain, as usual, handled the distribution process.

THE LARGE FRONT POCKETS OF HIS CAMOUFLAGE HUNTING COAT WERE chock-full of dried peanuts picked up from the field he was walking through, and his rifle was hanging loosely on his shoulder. A fence row ran parallel to the path on his right, and the hunter glanced casually in that direction ever so often as he ambled along, not a care in the world. He was on his way to the stand for an afternoon hunt, one that would surely be successful. Aren't they all, at least beforehand?

As he dug into a pocket for another double handful of goobers, he heard the classic bounding-on-cornflakes sound of a startled deer just across the fence. Sure enough, there was a whitetail, antlers and all, and before running off to the Siberian ski slopes, the buck pulled up and cast one last longing look at familiar surroundings. Large mistake. Fountain very promptly divested himself of the nuts, whipped the rifle into place, and sent a sizable chunk of lead whistling off into the wild blue yonder, in which direction the four-legged target had just gone, marching double time. Johnny was pretty sure the deer was hit in just the right spot, despite the fact that it disappeared quickly into some brush. A brief examination turned up a revealing red-tinted patch of hair, with the red very closely resembling the buck's blood type.

Our hero followed the trail through the weeds, strips of which had been bush-hogged down for better hunter visibility. He eventually emerged from a particularly nasty patch only to come eyeball-to-eyeball with a second deer, also bearing decidedly deciduous growths upon its noggin. It, too, struck the position peculiar to its klutzy clan, posing with head held high to present a perfect side brain shot, which was promptly executed.

We now have one down to stay and one to go. Johnny thought it all out, turned away from his present course and went in the opposite direction from which he thought the wounded deer would go, which is exactly the way it usually works.

Rambling around quite a while longer, he finally gave up and trudged half-heartedly back toward the truck . . . walking up on the first buck, dead as charity, en route.

This is not a lucky guy, or so he keeps telling me.

Later in the week, the pair of us spotted a female-type whitetail delicately brunching on our broad green soybeans. We happened to be heading hunting and cruising a field road in Old Blackie at the time. By the time the '65 was calmed down and ditched, literally, and we had donned our legally-required orange vests, loaded rifles, and gathered other totally unnecessary but always-toted gear, I figured the lass was at least a mile away.

But when Johnny, big-bore in hand, catfooted down the fence bordering the bean field, there she stood, chewing her cud like she owned the place. "Bust her! Bust her!" I urged.

"Let me get a rest first, then I will. She's a pretty good ways out there." He stomped weeds and he rattled and he fiddled, and she stood watching with mild interest all the while. Curiosity may well have killed the cat, and it does a pretty good job on female whitetails, too.

It was enough to give a hard-luck hunter like me the dry heaves. Man, I can exhale and spook a doe at a hundred paces! The only thing that prevented my accusing Johnny of being in league with evil forces was the ham and shoulder I got after the undressing process. Beggars can't be choosers.

OH, THERE HAVE BEEN SEVERAL BENEFICIARIES OF THIS HERD'S benevolence besides Fountain. I've been blessed on an occasion or twain, but at least I always felt I was a tad smarter than the herd. There was one fellow hunter, however, who was almost on their IQ level, at least early in his deer career. Despite the best intentions, advice, and hard work of several fellow hunters/instructors, Bud, as we'll call him, just couldn't seem to get the hang of things . . .

DAYLIGHT WAS ALREADY MAKING A FEEBLE ATTEMPT TO SHED A LITTLE LIGHT on things as Bud and I bounced the truck down the excuse for a road. Bud was doing his dead-level best not to miss any potholes, and was having uncanny success at it. Naturally, since we had escaped hard labor at the salt mines for a couple of days, it was drizzling rain and promising to be generally miserable until the exact instant when we clocked back in and pick and shovel were once again in hand. At that moment, the sun would rocket its way into a gorgeous blue sky and birds would plug in their own brand of stereo system right on cue. Never fails.

My driver and companion in arms had never killed a deer, and we had high hopes of rectifying that this morning. Rattling through the mud (most of the rattle came from our heads clanging off the truck cab), I happened to notice that Bud had missed a pothole. I was about to instruct him to back up and try again when it became apparent that his eyeballs were bugged approximately a foot in front of his skullbone. Following his wild-eyed stare, I could discern three flashes of white . . . you can probably guess . . . through the blackness of the pines.

The flashers proved to be just what we were looking for, and since they didn't seem to be seriously spooked, I thunk up a plan for heading one off at the proverbial pass. I, in infinite magnanimity and acute stupidity, would put Bud out here, motor on around the small, narrow, U-shaped stand of trees the deer were in, park and slog in toward them on foot, reasoning that they should be turned around and driven like, shall we say, sheep to slaughter. The plan worked to perfection. Almost.

I slogged in all right, managing to keep equally as dry as your average everyday carp. And the whiteys turned, moved slowly back from whence they had come and eased out right on schedule, into the clear with Bud standing not thirty yards away—shooting iron at the ready. Almost.

It seems that Bud was not all that familiar with the weapon. Although it had been in his possession for some time, he had never opened the box of .35-caliber bullets initially purchased with it until leaving the truck that morning. The gun is one of those like *Gunsmoke's* Festus Hagan carried in the scabbard as he tooled around Dodge City on his mule, Ruth. The weapon has a lever, a hammer, and a trigger, just like Festus's. Unlike his . . . we found out later . . . there's also a push-button safety on the side.

While Ol' Bud was growling like a starving lion and trying to figure out why his new toy wouldn't go "boom," the does decided they'd be better off in Outer Mongolia, toward which they headed as if late for a train. I was amused, to say the least, when I backstroked up and heard the un-gory details. "They went thataway," Bud said, just before I strangled him. Almost.

And here is the rest of the story . . .

While I, now molded into a shapeless lump of soggy camouflage, trekked onward to my nearby ladder stand, Bud trailed relentlessly after the aforementioned trio of ladies fair. I had not been settled in two minutes before the crash of a nearby rifle nearly caused me to become even wetter that I already was. Before my blood pressure reading could get back into triple digits, off went the .35 again. How 'bout that? Bud's learned how to make that gun shoot! Twice!

How, yes; but not where. There's a deer-hunting saying concerning rifle shots that goes something like, "One, down; two, maybe; three, running; four, gone." Hopping down all set to offer sincere congratulations . . . maybe . . . I roamed off to find Bud nearly as miserable as I had earlier been. Turns out he had found what he was looking for, but only after they had found a big-racked buck. The story came out in strangled gasps, but my fingers were miraculously not involved. Buck fever had struck again, and in spades. We found neither deer, hair, nor blood, only the torn-up areas where the foursome had whirled to run.

The reality of the situation was obvious: he had missed from twenty-five yards. And if you think that was bad shootin', consider the fact that he and another equally inept nimrod later in the week rattled off a couple of volleys in the general direction of half a herd of hustling whitetails who were busy battening down the hatches at full speed across an open field. The boys emptied two repeating rifles and never cut a hair on deer at less than a hundred yards. These guys can really shoot.

Almost.

21

THE UN-MACHO
DEER HUNTER

Outdoor writers such as Yours Faithfully are generally supposed to be able to instruct you on how to go about harvesting twelve-point bucks and larger to the point that you're able to pick, choose, and cull anything less. Prepare to go into your best Fred Sanford heart attack routine here because I am about to admit to a bit of personal heresy. Basically, I couldn't care less whether the deer in my crosshairs is male or female, horned or bald, on the dumb side or a Harvard graduate. I guess you could say I am the quintessential equal opportunity deer hunter. Over the last few years, there has been a growing number of like-minded un-macho guys feasting on some mighty fine red meat.

One of the basic reasons for this, especially in the real world below the Mason-Dixon Line, is that our whitetail herds are exploding. For instance, in my home state of Georgia, the number of deer when stocking first began in the 1950s was estimated at thirty-two thousand. The present herd is estimated, very conservatively I believe, at 1.2 million. It is imperative that we keep these numbers in check, to prevent the disaster of whitetail overpopulation and die-off from disease or mass starvation. After all, which is more humane, a hunter's bullet or the lingering, gnawing agony of going without food? Those of us who know her well can assure you that Mother Nature definitely has a dark side.

One of this world's classiest inhabitants is a former director of Georgia's Department of Natural Resources, Leon Kirkland. Despite the fact that he had a high government position and an office to match, Leon was never a stuffed shirt. Instead, he was and remains a hunter and lover of wildlife, which may sound a mite redundant to fellow members of the hunting fraternity. Especially close to my heart is the fact that Kirkland feeds a pack of rabbit-hounding beagles that have provided me with quite a few thrills as well as ink-stained recollections.

"As long as you're adequately harvesting your bucks, taking the does is the only real way to control the deer herd," Kirkland said of whitetail management. "We took about 90,000 of them in one season several years ago, then increased it to 130,000 the very next year. That's what it takes to keep things in check."

How and what you hunt is largely a matter of personal preference and game availability. But the whitetail deer is so well-established throughout North America that there's not much of a short supply within the reach of nearly any hunter. On our present hunting tracts, the members of my small (approximately two) group are currently in the process of thinning out the herd, and we have a definite order of shootees. First and foremost are big spike bucks, which tend to pass on their genetic shortcomings in short order. Then there are the does early in the season to fill the freezer, and small bucks, if an absolute necessity, to fill a tag late. As you may imagine, there is not too much passing-up of very large ten-pointers anywhere down the line, but we do go for the skinheads and small stuff when possible to let the bucks grow.

If we hunters don't manage our herds properly . . . and yes, it is up to us . . . we're going to be seeing "big" deer tipping the scales at around one hundred pounds and panhandling on every street corner. Just for purposes of comparison, the heaviest deer ever taken in Georgia tipped the scales at an almost unbelievable 335 pounds field-dressed, tying it with a Maine whitetail as the second-heaviest ever recorded. Number one is a Minnesota deer taken in 1926, an incredible 402-pounder, field-dressed. Another interesting fact about Boyd Jones's record Georgia buck, killed in Worth County in 1972, is that it is the descendant of a herd of Wisconsin whitetails. They were purchased by a hardy group of farmers and hunters who paid their own hard-earned 1950s cash to transport and stock a total of ninety-six live deer from Wisconsin on their own, without state assistance. Their efforts paid off with an almost pure strain of Wisconsin whitetails that produces among the largest and, obviously, heaviest bucks in the world. It just goes to show what a group of hunters can do when they set their minds to something.

That our southern herd has grown to dangerous propor-tions, regardless of the preservationists' ranting that Bambi is just now perched on two hooves upon the brink of extinction, is evidenced by the ease in which some fellow hunters and I recently filled our tags. For the first four days of the past season alone, I saw twenty-three deer within slingshot range. One of them was an eight-pointer that streaked, just one step slow, across a cornfield corner. He was one of only two bucks, the other being a button-variety job that is probably still wondering where the brief rain came from. (I had a sudden urge to rid myself of a mouthful of moisture just as he passed under my tree stand, and never a more startled deer have you seen.) The other twenty-one had nothing between the ears, either on top of or inside their skulls, as near as I can figure.

One red-letter morning, Fountain and I piddled around until 9:30 in the A.M., a habit of ours, before taking to the woods. Please do not delude yourself into believing that being up an oak tree an hour before daylight is absolutely necessary. I've killed many more deer along about the middle of the morning than at dawn, and so has my partner. Besides, I'm basically lazy when it comes to crawling out of bed at 5:00 A.M. on a Saturday, and Fountain got off work at eight. All in all, things work out fairly well.

He drove me to an old logging road that pretty much halved a morass of scrub oaks, briars, pushed-up trees of all kinds and, last but not least, planted pines eight feet high. I would give him five minutes to drive around and park, then would walk in as he did from the other side, hopefully catching something wearing unshod hooves between us. Perhaps "creep" is a better word to use than "walk." I've still-hunted with guys who seemed to think it was halftime of a college football game and they were wearing bearskin hats, white boots, and carrying batons for all the ease in which they traversed the woods. As an aside, these guys are perfectly grand to use on a deer drive or a rabbit stomp, because they send anything within hearing range, roughly a two-square-mile area, your way.

When Johnny and I still-hunt, snails routinely whiz by hurrying along on daily errands, and the only noise is made by eyeballs swishing through the brush. This particular path has a slight bend to the left in it which then opens up to a fifty-yard straightaway, and just before getting to that special spot, I inadvertently crunched a leaf under my left boot. When this happens, the first order of business is to freeze, no matter what position you're in. This was duly undertaken. Then, because I have made a sound, any sound at all, I silently remind myself that I am cerebrally ranked just below an orangutan.

While doing my best imitation of granite, a movement ahead called attention to a young but nicely-filled-out doe, tripping across the way. Two more materialized, as only white-tails can do, behind her. Let's see now, eeny, meeny, miney, boom! Shouldering and shooting that old rifle has become almost as automatic as throwing up a shotgun, so there was no worry about the shot at a range of twenty-five yards. But strange things, such as, "I wonder how high Johnny's gonna jump?" ran through my mind just before pulling the trigger.

I never did find out, but the doe did go pretty high. Well, at least her hind feet did as she kicked like a mule . . . a sure sign of a heart shot . . . before kicking into overdrive. She bolted about twenty feet, then piled up stone dead. One of the remaining deer skittered into the trees, but the third wandered around like a lonesome country girl in Times Square. After watching her smallish self through the crosshairs for thirty seconds or so, I decided to let her grow. Five minutes into the hunt, it's Visitors 1, Home Team 0.

Fountain drove back around and we loaded this one onto the truck, then rolled on another five hundred or so yards through the woods. We were mostly just lookin' and talkin', and then we recalled a nearby three-year-old tree stand of two-by-fours that needed checking for safety and sign of nearby whitetail activity. Some one hundred feet into the trees, with Fountain waiting outside in a barren field by the truck, we carried on a conversation concerning the boards, limbs, and overall construction of stands in general. All that distance apart, we made absotively no attempt at being quiet. Inspection completed, I began rambling back toward the field . . . only to hear the old familiar sound of four feet rapidly hitting the ground just ahead.

I froze, then eased the Remington to shoulder level in minute movements. But my view was blocked by thick stuff, so I cat-footed back around the tree to see what was going on. After all, we may be invited to the party.

Up ahead, believe it or not, were three more dense deer, one a very large doe eyeballing me like she thought my plans didn't fit her schedule. Right you are, darlin', and I touched things off again. This time, Johnny, who had also heard the initial proceedings and was intently peering through his own scope trying to pick out a target, admitted to coming within centimeters of the world high jump record, and from a squatting position no less.

The stuff between her and me was so thick that I had an opening of only a foot or so to put a bullet through, but there was no doubt. If the blood trail on the first she-male was impressive, this one was downright unbelievable, with an initial spray that would cover an average non-import car hood. This doe, almost twice as large as the first, didn't go half as far.

The reason I mention the red-tinted details is because of a new bullet I had recently become enamored of. Being your average deer hunter, and claiming to be no more, I'm not much on touting one product over another, and I certainly reap no reward from doing so. But I have been so impressed with the 165-grain variety of .30-06 that the load bears mention. My first box of the bad boys was purchased at a mini-auction during a gathering of outdoor writers at Jack Wingate's Lunker Lodge on Lake Seminole. I wanted a second, but so did Leon Kirkland, and he makes more money than I do.

For years, I had used a 150-grain bullet, a fine one in its own right. But in my humble opinion these extra fifteen grains of fisticuffs have no equal. The first three 165s I touched off killed, in order, a tremendous red wolf in Ontario and these two deer. Since then, they have proved themselves equally as effective. Single-shot kills are what hunting is all about, and it's hard to argue with success. If you do not roll your own brand of homogenized load, opting for the factory gender, give this one a try.

As if the previous episode wasn't enough to sway us on the availability of wandering venison, let us now say thanks to whomever moved the ladder stand from the corner oak to the middle of the wilderness, unbeknownst to anyone but himself.

You know how it is about a certain sure-fire, can't-miss location you've never seen: "Go into the edge of the trees at the left corner of the field, walk twenty paces straight toward the third fence post and it's right there on that big oak. You can't miss it."

Wanna bet? Most of the time, I've found that I couldn't find one of these spots with a detailed pirate map, two sextants, three compasses, and a patch-eyed guide. Problem is, usually when you go looking it's before daylight and about as dark as the inside of a cow. A "friend" of mine gave me an exact location of one of these places shortly after I had become acquainted with those two lately lamented and very tasty missies. They had relatives; what I had was a good friend who had placed me on a reputed dove field that turned out to be a sure-enough dove field. He was owed, so he was along.

As we stomped and peered through the darkness, we knew it had to be here, cussit, somewhere! Trails around this alleged stand looked like your run-of-the-mill cattle drive had just come through, but there was no ladder to be located. Dawn was coming on, so we were not exactly in the frame of mind such as upon tax-refund morn.

Oh well, there was definitely a good spot a hundred yards away, one which overlooked a pair of scrapes and a regular elk-variety rub. I selfishly wanted to hold it out for myself, but the bills had to be paid. Ol' Big Boy would certainly frolic by within thirty minutes after sunrise, so I'd place Partner there. Then I would go find that lost ladder stand, all the way questioning the ancestry and right to life of its mover.

"Light is coming on," I tell myself after my friend was in place. "Better sit your frozen butt down, boy."

A scrub oak had bit the dust maybe a month before and was now resting bentover with its foot-thick trunk three feet off the dirt. When the birds and squirrels started complaining, I knew it was time to squat, so I eased between the limbs and onto the trunk of the fallen tree. Ten minutes passed, as uncomfortable as I can remember, before three deer simply walked up unannounced. They absolutely materialized out of thin air, as whitetails so often do.

Now there are times when I enjoy sitting and watching deer just to see how they react to certain things and what they do in general as they're wandering around.

But this wasn't one of them.

A particularly obese female was subsequently presented with just over a hundred and a half grains of high-powered diet program, and her worldly binging problems were over. That's when things got even more interesting. The big-bore rifle is a loud commodity in any class, but in the foggy dawn the .30-06 is probably teacher's pet. Big Gal didn't hear a thing, but I fully expected the other pair to go crashing off like a couple of juvenile avalanches. Following a brief hop-scotch routine or two, however, they turned right around and returned to the scene of the crime. Go figure!

Weighing options . . . to burn another tag or not to burn another tag . . . the decision was made to issue a blast in the direction of the other big 'un. Venison is, as they say, venison, and never a better tasting morsel will scorch human lips. With the shot, a little-finger-sized limb that hadn't shown up in the scope came flying off the side of a tree between us, and the bullet chunked off another tree just above and behind her. That, my friend, changed things considerably.

She kicked up a minor gale while streaking off, and my only wish is that there had been some way of clocking her speed when she hit wide-open. The other one? She never even moved as far as I could tell, right up until I eased over to begin carving on supper. Even then, she stayed around to make sure I found my way, departing only upon my arrival.

You hunters want a word of advice about these freaky females? Well here it is: bust 'em if you get the chance!

22

TROPHIES, SURE-ENOUGH

E very deer hunter has seen at least one of those monstrous male whitetails with the rocking-chair rack and thought to himself, "If only I could get a shot at one of those. . . ." The problem with seeing them is that they're usually on someone's else's wall or in some taxidermist's shop. Somewhere down the line, in every hunter's mind, is one buck that stands out far above the rest. So it is with me.

Unfortunately, this one isn't on my wall, either. It belongs to Elliott Harrison, and at six-foot-six and tipping the scales at more than seventeen stone, Elliott is not one you'd try to take it away from. Besides nearly causing cardiac arrest the first time I ever laid eyes on it, the rack came equally as close to making the Boone and Crockett Club's revered listings. That it didn't is B&C's loss, because I've seen many book racks that don't come close to being as impressive as this one. Here's the first of two live-and-in-color episodes in which a deer hunter's dream comes true.

THE NOVEMBER MORNING DAWNED GRAY AND RAINY, BUT HARRISON didn't mind. He had it in his head that he was going deer hunting this day and nothing would deter him. "Besides," he reasoned, "a little sprinkle never hurt anybody; in fact, it just might help."

Many times before he had seen showers touch off activity among whitetails in the area he hunted. Harrison was optimistic, yes, but he had no idea that just before the cloudy gloom snuffed out the last of the afternoon's light, his bullet would bring down the buck bearing the biggest non-typical rack killed in Georgia during the season.

Harrison hails from the small town of Montrose, some fifteen miles from my home in Dublin, Georgia, in Laurens County. He has hunted here since the inception of our season in the mid-1960s. That first year, he brought down his first buck, a single-antlered animal equipped with only the left side of its rack, which featured five points. Since that time, Harrison has failed to take the legal limit of deer only one season, and he had good reasons for that: an auto accident that laid him up, followed by the death of his father.

Just on the north side of Turkey Creek . . . and it seems that every county in America has a Turkey Creek . . . Harrison began his love affair with the whitetail. Since that time, he has learned bundles both about and from his quarry. That knowledge paid off on an overcast November day when he killed a buck that scored 187 and seven-eighths Boone and Crockett points. The minimum score for inclusion within the hallowed pages of the B&C record book for non-typicals is 195, so he missed by seven and an eighth. One look at this mount, though, and one could not possibly care less about a book listing. It's kind of like kicking Raquel Welch out of bed on a cold winter night simply because she was never named Miss America.

The living room in Harrison's home features three mounted deer heads. As one enters the front door, directly ahead on the wall are two very impressive eight-pointers. But something always seems to beckon the peepers just a little to the left, to the small area over the television set. Actually, the space is not small at all; it just looks that way because there is one monstrous whitetail dominating everything else in sight . . . which has been promptly forgotten.

The rack commands the full attention and awe of all who enter. Hanging beside it is a plaque from the Southeastern Buckarama, the largest deer-hunting show in the U.S. of A., which attests to its number one ranking for the year's non-typical bucks. There's a story behind that, too, but let's get back to the day of the hunt.

"I got up and hunted that morning despite the clouds, but didn't see anything," Harrison recalls. "I came in about dinnertime and went back out later in the afternoon. I had heard some deer in this area before, but hadn't seen any. In fact, I had allowed some people to hunt from the very stand I killed the big buck from, but they hadn't seen anything, either."

Harrison hunts exclusively from ladder stands, which he has erected at strategic locations throughout his hunting range. This particular one was less than a mile from his home, and approximately a mile-and-a-half from Interstate 16 in Laurens County.

"I was more or less scouting around when I went back that afternoon," the hunter continues, "when I heard some deer down in the woods. They sounded like they were fighting, because I could hear antlers clashing together and limbs snapping. They were probably a good two hundred yards from me, but I could hear them well. I know the distance, because they were splashing in water at times, and the only water around is a beaver pond in there."

When he heard the bucks battling, Harrison immediately eased closer to them, then spotted his ladder stand and climbed in. Thirty minutes later, the buck of a lifetime materialized from the darkening depths of the hardwoods. The stand was mounted on an oak, on the edge of a large soybean field.

As the light faded, Harrison desperately hoped the buck would move out of the shadows and into the field.

"I guess the bucks fought their way up the hill toward me, and they didn't pay any attention to the noise I made going up the stand," Harrison remarked. "One thing that was in my favor was that the wind was blowing directly from them toward me."

That wind undoubtedly made the difference, because when the buck finally walked out to the border of the beans, he was facing directly toward the hunter and some seventy-five yards away. A whitetail buck can tell what brand of deodorant you're using and what size can it came out of from two hundred yards. With any sign at all of man scent on the breeze, this one would never have entered the field. At the very least, the animal would have been alerted to some degree by his radar nose, and would likely have picked out the man holding the rifle.

But even when the buck took a couple more steps, the field didn't offer an awful lot of light.

"At first I couldn't see any antlers. I could see a deer, but I couldn't tell if it was one of the bucks or maybe the doe they had been fighting over. I finally noticed it was a buck when I saw one of the drop tines. I couldn't see any of the upward-reaching tines, but when he tossed his head around and bent down to eat some beans, I could tell he had a heavy rack."

After a first glance at that "heavy rack," one would wonder how Harrison could possibly have missed it. But as every hunter who has been in a similar position knows, shadows can play havoc with the eyes, especially in a case such as this with fading light and surging adrenalin factored into the equation. It goes to show the level of competence and plain old good hunting sense of the man that he waited until he was absolutely sure at what he would be shooting.

That hard-to-see rack, by the way, is what could be classified as a seventeen-pointer, with ten points on one side, seven on the other. It has a twenty-five-inch inside spread, with the longest single tine being the drop tine on the right, which was measured at eight and seven-eighths inches.

"He was standing in some thick weeds," Harrison continued, "and I let him move on out into the field a little farther. I could see it was a monster buck, and I didn't want to take any chances." Then, of course, Harrison had to contend with the usual problem deer hunters face when a trophy whitetail is anywhere in the neighborhood: wrong side. In other words, he would have to turn all the way around on the stand.

"I'm right-handed and he was on my right. I sure didn't want to take a chance shooting at him left-handed. My heart was pounding so hard I was hardly able to hold the gun. I was almost as worried that he'd hear my heart as I was that he'd hear me move. When I finally got into position, I shot for the heart the first time, and he broke and ran. I thought for an instant I had missed him, but the scope had gathered enough light to pretty well let me call my shot. As he ran in front of me, he started slowing down, so I knew he was hit. He was headed for the woods, though, and I didn't want him to get there, so I shot him again."

As the Remington .30-06 roared the second time, the buck piled up in a heap, brick dead when he hit the ground. The bullet had snapped the spine, and the buck of a lifetime belonged to Elliott Harrison.

"When I first walked up to him, I couldn't believe that rack!" the hunter said, awe still evident in his voice. "It looked like it was knee-high . . . and he was lying flat." Remembering Elliott's size, we realize that knee-high is a pretty good ways up.

It was 5:30 in the afternoon, and getting dark fast, when Harrison realized he had a problem. "I like to have never found my deer tags," he said with a wry grin. "I was scared to move the deer without tagging it and I knew I had the things somewhere. I went through my billfold three or four times before I ever found them, but there they were."

State law, by the way, requires that animals be properly tagged before they are moved from the kill site. Failure to do so can, and does, result in fines and, even worse, seizure of the deer. Wearing a gun and badge or not, I would hate to have known that it was my job to confiscate that particular buck!

Montrose is a small, close-knit community where everybody knows everybody. It didn't take long for the word to get out after Harrison had made it home with his trophy.

"I've never had as many people at my house at one time as I did the night I killed that deer. Some of my friends dressed it for me. It was so big that they thought it was an honor just to get to gut it. I was so excited that after I went to work that night at midnight, I had to call my wife to see if I had left any of the gates open to the back soybean field where the buck was killed. I had cows back there, and I knew they'd be scattered everywhere if any gates were left open." Even in his excitement, however, Harrison had managed to close them all.

The trophy animal weighed just over 195 pounds, and it was clear that he was in the rut, with other things besides food on his mind. Taxidermists who mounted the head estimated the age at just over five years, putting the deer in its prime. Despite the buck's age, neither Harrison nor any of his fellow hunters had ever seen it.

The taxidermists also urged Harrison to enter the head in a big deer contest, which he did. The first prize was a Ruger Mini-14 rifle. Although the buck took top honors, the gun wasn't presented right away. Harrison's wife, Edith, took the phone-call notification that the head had won, and decided to spring a surprise at the Buckarama. Harrison didn't find out about his new ordnance until the day it was presented to him.

The taking of this buck was the culmination of years of hard hunting for the Montrose hunter, and it would be a shame if we didn't get to share some of his expertise. Although he had never seen this particular animal, Harrison knew there were bucks of considerable size roaming the area on which he hunts. He knows the woods and fields intimately, and that fact contributed greatly to the prime placement of that stand and, ultimately, the harvesting of the trophy itself. The surrounding terrain includes some of his favorite hunting spots.

"I like to hunt mostly down in the woods, away from everybody else," he says. "First off, I look for signs of deer activity, such as scrapes, rubs, droppings, and such."

Harrison said he checks out a prospective area closely before opening day, and that's it. "I go into the tract about a month before the season opens, make my plans, set up a ladder stand, then get out. I won't go back until opening day at the earliest. If I've set up several stands, which I usually do, I may not hit it for a couple of weeks after the season opens.

"Some of my favorite places to hunt are hardwood bottomlands, especially with creeks nearby. When it comes to fields, there's only one kind to hunt over as far as I'm concerned, and that's soybeans. I'd really rather set up a stand a little ways back in the trees near a bean field and catch the deer on the way in. They're usually not as alert there as they are once they've entered an open field."

And there's one more place Harrison prefers, a special favorite.

"Beaver ponds are real good to hunt over, too, and I don't know why. Lots of times I've heard deer splashing around in them and I've killed several near those ponds. I've also seen bucks cross shallow water to small islands in the middle of the ponds and bed down."

So what does one do for an encore after downing a buck such as this one? Well, there's a matter of just over seven B&C points that bugs him.

"One of my goals since I've been deer hunting is to put a buck in the Boone and Crockett record book. I've always looked forward to doing that, and I really thought this one was it. But the rack actually cost me some points being a nontypical. There are some other good deer left around here, though, and I'd like to check them out."

He held up a single shed antler picked up while scouting, an absolutely immense, perfectly-formed five-pointer, and said with a grin, "I'd like to see what dropped this. And don't forget, the seventeen-pointer was fighting just before I took him. I'd sure like to see what chased him to that soybean field."

IF ELLIOTT HARRISON SEEMED TO HAVE STUMBLED ONTO HIS TROPHY, AND maybe got a little lucky, well, that's deer hunting. So, too, is the story of David Frost's buck. Frost lucked onto, in a manner of speaking, what every bright-eyed deerslayer dreams of: a record-book buck. He lucked onto it all right; trouble was, it was three years of hard work later before Frost was able to formally introduce the big boy to his livingroom wall. Here's how it happened . . .

EARLY-MORNING MIST ROSE COOLLY AND SERENELY FROM THE SWAMPY bottomland along the Oconee River, in Wheeler County very near the Laurens County line, as Frost's boots squished and padded softly through the dark, rich mud. He was going through the motions of his usual still-hunting methods, unaware that within seconds a three-year crusade for the animal of a lifetime would begin; or that his life would be changed forever and his name included in that little book belonging to Messrs. Boone and Crockett.

And it all started with an ear.

The mosquito-discouraging flip caught his eye as Frost was almost on top of some kind of deer or other. As he suddenly made like a tree, his heart pumping by the gallon, the doe that belonged to that ear shrugged him off and resumed her browsing. Within seconds, the hunter was able to make out the forms of a couple more deer ghosting through the woods.

One member of the second party was a female for sure, but Frost couldn't tell enough about the third until he had eased up the rifle and counted its neck hairs through the big scope. No doe day, no shot; all in all, he thought it was pretty disgusting to see all those deer and not even get a bruised shoulder. Pulling the rifle down, Frost figured he'd watch a while, at least until something caught sight or scent of him and headed for Greece at a gallop.

That's when the splashing started.

Really fired up now, David scoured the bottom for what was making all the racket. Spotting her . . . HER! . . . he heaved another sigh of disgust. But she was not alone. What happened next touched off countless thousands of hours of wondering, waiting and, most of all, hoping, over a three-year span. Because trailing that big doe was the largest whitetail buck David Frost will probably ever see. The four-legged dude very obviously had lovin' and nothing else on his mind as he chased the female, but she was having nothing to do with him. For those who are uninformed when it comes to the basics of making little whitetails, what it boils down to is that he was chasing her until she caught him. The process was about to be loudly interrupted, however.

Neither of the lovey-doveys noticed Frost, but the range and terrain were such that he was able to touch off only a single hurried shot at the trotting buck.

He missed.

"I know I didn't hit him and he just left the area for the rest of that season. It was as simple as that; he disappeared completely. I just about lived in there hoping to get another chance, but he didn't show up."

You dedicated deer hunters know what it's like to get up before first light morning after morning, then perch upon your painful posterior until the shadows take over each night. But what if you had seen and taken a shot at such a buck? What if . . .

Frost managed to take a nice eight-pointer in the same neighborhood, but it was to be Thanksgiving Day of the next year before his dream of seeing the monster buck again was realized.

"That Thanksgiving, I had gone into the woods with my daddy, and the wind got up real bad about nine in the morning.

I got up to start stalking and had walked about ten yards when I heard something behind me.

"I whirled around, heard him snort, and caught a glimpse of him running flat out through the woods. I sighted on an opening, but he came through so fast that I didn't have a good shot, and I certainly didn't want to risk wounding and losing him. I could see his big old rack bouncing through the woods, and I was sick. I felt like throwing the gun down and quitting right then and there."

Do you get the feeling that Frost is one dedicated deer hunter? I wonder how many of us would have passed up that piece of a shot. Throwing down the gun and quitting was not Frost's way, however, and the sick feeling didn't last long either. While he was agonizing over whether or not he should have risked a pop at the big'un, a silly little five-pointer came trotting up and was promptly transformed into table fare.

"I'll always believe that the big buck sent that little one right to me," Frost says. At any rate, it had to make things just a little better on that particular trip. But the wondering and waiting continued for yet another year.

It was Thanksgiving Day again, and Frost had discovered a series of rubs and scrapes that he said could only have been made by the monster buck. It was time for drastic measures, so the hunter who had never used a tree-top special decided to bring a ladder stand into the area. It would be his first time in an elevated stand of any type. It would also be a very memorable one.

Frost clambered in well before daylight. An hour later, at 7:15, he heard splashing in the same creek that he had seen the buck cross during that first sighting so long ago. Moments later, as the magnificent animal materialized from the mist, Frost knew that he was about to go home one extremely happy hunter . . . or take strike three.

Fate, be not tempted thrice.

Fortunately, the buck was coming toward him at an angle, on its way to presenting a perfect crossing shot. But for a moment the hunter thought Murphy's Law was going to come into play. The deer angled steadily toward the very wading spot the hunter had taken on the way to the stand. Surely, its super sniffer was about to pick up the feared and hated scent . . . and it surely did.

The animal pulled up short like a setter on point as it caught a whiff. As Mother Nature would have it, buck was looking directly at rifleman. That one moment of indecision loomed large as the Marlin roared. Incredibly, the deer took off without even a flinch, and Frost's old familiar sick feeling returned with a vengeance.

"I thought I had missed him by the way he acted, even though that scope's crosshairs were right where I wanted them. I had sighted it in just that week. I tried to put a sight on him twice more as he was running, touched off two more quick shots . . . and missed both of them."

The forlorn hunter watched in agony as the buck barreled through the trees. But when it went to cross the creek again in a giant leap, David's heart soared even as the whitetail's gave out. With a tremendous splash, the buck crashed into the water. The bullet had done its duty. It was recovered from the deer's heart during the dressing-out process.

The huge non-typical rack scored 198 and four-eighths Boone and Crockett points. The most interesting point was a drop tine on the right side which was covered in hardened velvet. It was mounted that way and remains on Frost's wall today.

One wonders what's next for a man who has killed a record-book buck, especially after a three-year hunt that ended in glory.

"I don't know if there's one in that swamp that's bigger," Frost says, "but I've seen one that comes pretty close."

Makes you wonder how many years this one's going to take!

23

TROUBLES HAVEN'T TRAPPED JEFF

The moon is still a shivering sliver, icy in its whiteness and solitude, as Jeff Hutcheson slowly brings himself to full consciousness. The bed's warmth is tempting for a sleep-dulled moment, but there's a trapline to be run. And the job won't get done from here.

Hauling himself out, Hutcheson hurriedly bundles up against the biting cold and heads outside into the darkness. His trusty golf cart, in all its camouflaged glory, looms up out of the gloom, and he climbs in.

"Checking traps from a golf cart?" you ask.

No, it's not that Hutcheson is too lazy to walk. In fact, there's nothing on the face of the earth that he'd enjoy more. The problem, you see, is that he can't. Hutcheson is paralyzed from the waist down and, to use the common and detested term, "confined" to a wheelchair. But anyone who has spent any time at all around this guy will quickly inform you that he is anything but confined. And his great love for hunting, fishing, trapping, and the outdoors in general is a

148

major force behind his drive back to mobility.

The golf cart, like his four-wheel-drive SUV, is equipped with hand controls, and the huddled trapper rolls quickly through biting wind and into the shelter of swaying pines behind his Middle Georgia home. On this morning, the ride is both frigid and fruitful. The sets contain several foxes and a 'coon, each handled quickly and efficiently as Hutch makes the rounds. Near the end of the line, he hears a rowdy commotion from the direction of one of his traps. As the cart rattles up, its motor whirring softly, the trapper feels a burning surge as he spies the source of all the racket.

A large and definitely displeased bobcat, one hind leg gripped firmly by the trap, is undertaking a radical redecoration of the limited portion of countryside within his reach. A .22-caliber dose of a rather powerful sedative is quickly administered, and the feline calms down considerably. (For occasions when that dosage is not quite strong enough, there is a backup syringe of sorts fully-equipped with a nine-inch needle and a .44-magnum nametag.)

The cat is a big one, and Hutch can't suppress a grin as he envisions the fighting-pose mount it will make when the local taxidermist gets his very talented hands on it.

Yessir, it's been a good morning so far. But it hasn't always been that way for Jeff.

IT WAS JUNE 10, 1982, A SWELTERING AFTERNOON, AND THE SEVENTEEN-year-old was still on an emotional high ten days after graduating from high school. As he playfully wheeled his dirt bike around the country roads and rolling fields surrounding his home, little did he know that before the day was over, nothing would ever be the same again.

Exactly what happened remains a little hazy. One moment the motorcycle was jumping back and forth over ditches and logs, and the next Hutcheson woke up with his face in the dirt, unable to turn over or even move an arm. He lay that way on the lonely road, in blistering sunshine and misery, for several hours, until a neighbor finally found him. Sensible enough not to risk moving the youngster, the rescuer quickly summoned an ambulance. The attendants scooped the youth up, dirt and all, and sped him to a hospital twenty miles away.

From there, he was moved to a larger hospital in a larger town; and to a still-larger one in a still-larger city. The fourth stop, after near-total paralysis was discovered, was the Shepherd Spinal Clinic in Atlanta. What happened over the next three months at Shepherd, and later back home, is a testament to the incredible mental and physical toughness of an extremely likable, friendly gentleman and his family. He has been, and is daily, an inspiration in my life and those of many others.

When physical therapy started, Hutch had no use at all of his legs and very limited motion in his upper body, arms, and hands. In the beginning, he could lift a grand total of five pounds with both hands. This from a kid who was six-foot five and, before the accident, was knocking on two hundred pounds and as strong as a bow-legged ox. But now, he lifted that five pounds over and over, monotonously, almost endlessly.

Soon it grew to ten pounds, then twenty. Fifty. A hundred. Now, his upper body resembles that of a gorilla, and he shoves two hundred pounds of iron around like he owns it. Hands that once were beginning to take on the classic curved, claw-like condition of unused limbs now nimbly whip six-pound-test line through the eyes of bream hooks. Hutch spent three grueling months at Shepherd, coming home in September. All in all, it was almost as if the whole episode was a very unpleasant little vacation. As always, Hutch downplays any mention of the agonies of that summer.

"The worst thing about it is that I didn't have much of a summer break. When I got home from the clinic, I started college almost immediately, and it was back to the same old grind."

This, remember, comes from a guy who has been told that he will never walk again . . . an assertion he steadfastly refuses to believe. Knowing him as I do, I don't much believe it either. But there were hard times by the bushel basketful, a few shed tears, and more than a little pain behind those words of bravado. It was the spirit of Jeff Hutcheson, and indeed the entire family, that pulled him through.

"We never showed Jeff much sympathy, no matter how bad we wanted to," said his father, James. "We all knew it was going to be tough . . . that he was going to have to make it on his own. I couldn't be more pleased now with Jeff's attitude, and his ability to do just about anything he wants. His mother (Sue) is as responsible as anyone or anything else for his rehabilitation and outlook."

The elder Hutcheson's next statements give a little insight into just how the family treated the entire affair, realizing that laughter is, at times, the best medicine. "About the only thing Jeff can't do is walk, and I think he's decided rolling is easier anyway. He's good to ride with too, when he's driving, because he always gets the best parking places."

Sue Hutcheson, a woman whose loveliness conceals the effects of more than her share of tragedy, echoes her husband's sentiments.

"I think Jeff did most of it on his own, because he knew he had to," she says with a wistful look at the mention of painful memories. "But it took a lot of willpower . . . and a lot of clashing of wills."

While the injured youngster was at Shepherd, so, too, was his mother, training for the days when her near-helpless son would come home. She remembers those first few days back within the friendly confines of home very, very well.

"When Jeff first came back, he couldn't do anything for himself, so I had to do it for him. It was, as you can imagine, a very sad time, but we really had some knock-down, drag-outs, too. For example, I had to dress him, but I also had to teach him to dress himself. Even something as routinely simple as putting on his pants was a chore. He'd say 'I can't do it,' and I'd throw his pants down, stalk out, and leave him. It might

take him thirty minutes . . . which time I'd been in the bathroom crying, but he never knew . . . to put his pants on."

But he would do it.

Hour by hour, day by day, the ordeal went oh-so-slowly-
but-surely by. Eventually, the dividends began to show.

"There was another time, after he was in his wheelchair
and had just started to drive his car, when he couldn't get his
(collapsible) chair in the car with him," she recalls. "Again, he
said he just couldn't do it, so I told him that if he didn't want
to get it in, just to leave it sitting there. His grandmother was
there and she simply couldn't stand to watch and not help. But
she knew the situation, so she got in her own car and left."

So there they all were: Jeff halfway in and halfway out of his
specially-modified Pontiac Trans Am, his wheelchair resting
comfortably on the spanking-new concrete ramp leading from
the garage door, grandmother heading down the driveway in
tears, mother retreating to her bathroom sanctuary.

It was to be a turning point in his life.

"By the way," Sue smiles, "he got it in there after an awful
lot of clanging and banging went on out in the garage. Then he
peeled that car off down the road with the tires smoking . . .
before turning around, coming back, and apologizing. Now, he
throws that chair in and out like a sack of salt. I did things for
him then; from that point on, he has done for me."

Not showing Hutch any sympathy may have been the
master plan, but there is another episode in particular . . .
which his father may not even be aware of . . . that had a
lasting impact on his oldest son's future.

"When I came home in September, dove season was about
to open," Hutch says. "Daddy, Jason, and John (Jeff's younger
brothers) suited up, got down their guns, and walked out,
leaving me without a word. I made up my mind right then that
they'd never do it again."

(As if the family had not seen enough tragedy already, just
thirteen months after Jeff's accident, middle son Jason was
killed in an automobile crash.)

Now, not a hunting season goes by that doesn't find Jeff afield. He shoots doves either from his golf cart or from a light wheelchair, which he says provides better camouflage and an open front for swinging his scattergun. But he adds that the limitations of the golf cart provide good excuses when he misses! He has built himself a boat that has helped account for the demise of mallards and woodies all across the South, and during deer season, the golf cart is again called into use.

Let me tell you about my first trip in that contraption. Believe me, it was some ride.

Deep in his heart, Hutch believes he's stock car racing's finest driver. Or maybe he just gets a kick out of seeing his riders in abject terror as they leave imprints of their clutching fingers in the iron supports of his cart. At any rate, before you crawl in, be absolutely sure that your life insurance premiums are up to date and double indemnity is in effect, even though your demise may not be totally accidental.

The first morning I slid into the frozen seat of the cart, we went bouncing through the pines at roughly . . . and I do not use the term loosely . . . the speed of light. Despite my series of totally terrified pleas, protestations, and threats, Hutch never removed the pedal from the metal until we reached the junction of our journey known, in barest simplicity, as "The Hole." Believe me, this is a misnomer, not to mention understatement, if ever there was one. As we teetered upon the brink, either pity or Hutch's good upbringing took over, and the goggle-eyed driver graciously asked if I'd care to vacate the premises before he undertook the negotiation of said hole. Would I ever, and several hundred yards back, too!

But as you know, I've seen real mudholes before, and this spot very closely resembled what the Okefenokee Swamp would look like if it slid off into the Grand Canyon. There was a gleam in his eyes as Hutch raced full speed down the canyon wall, barreled into the swamp with mud and water flying, then went up the other side . . . sideways for the most part . . .

screaming like a constipated panther as the vehicle's wheels spun wildly. As miraculous as it may sound, he made it, and to Hutch that's all that counted. Even more miraculous was the fact that I stuck with him on the return trip . . . a master mistake for which I remain highly medicated.

We didn't find a bobcat in the sets on that morning, which was a blessing because I don't believe my heart could have taken any further stress; the old pump stopped several times and had to be jump-started as it was. Each time the fainting spells occured, Hutch would revive me with the private concoction he uses to scent his traps' pork-rind baits. He dips the pork in this stuff, and although a whiff of it up close would cross a skunk's eyes, predators such as bobcat and fox seem to find it divine.

Somewhere along the way, on that first outing, I fell in love with this kid. Don't worry; my wife understands. It is the kind of love that only men who are hunters and fishermen and campers and trappers and sufferers of great hurt in their lives can share. We have gone places and done things together from southern Georgia to northern Ontario, with never a cross word passed. Oh, what fine times we have had . . .

One of the early outings was a fishing trip, and I, in infinite ignorance, had no idea at all about the guy's limitations . . . which happen to be very few . . . or his abilities, which are vast. There was one rather awkward moment that set the tone for our entire relationship. It, too, gives great insight into how Hutch has handled things since his accident. As I prepared to clamber into the boat, it suddenly hit me that he had to get in also.

"Uh, how do you manage to get aboard?" I asked in profound innocence.

"Easy; you pick me up and carry me," came the offhand reply. So, as gently as a mother handles her newborn babe, I hefted this very large young'un and proceeded to do just that. When I had gotten to boatside, I was still fearful that my heavy-handedness might inflict some injury. Sensing my anxiety,

Hutch spouted, "There's just one rule you have to know about carrying me: if we fall, I land on top."

Laughing out of sheer relief, I almost dropped him into the water. But that wouldn't have been any great catastrophe since he can swim like a shark, although I didn't know that at the time, either. From that moment to this, we have gotten along famously.

Fish? He can catch 'em when I couldn't boat one with dynamite. Hunt? Well, it's like this archery kick he's gotten on.

When it comes to hunting with bow and arrow, Hutch is severely handicapped. His physical condition doesn't have a thing to do with that, because it is my unequivocal opinion that anyone who uses a string and a sharp stick to try to kill something as tough as a whitetail is severely handicapped from the outset. You've heard the proverbial "couldn't hit a bull in the butt with a bass fiddle?" That's about the way I am with a bow. We're talking about missing the barn wall from inside the barn.

But Hutch? Well, let his father tell this story . . .

"Jeff had driven his golf cart into the edge of a field, and watched this doe make her way out of the bordering woods. She meandered up to within fifty feet of him and he shot. The arrow went in perfectly just behind the shoulder. The deer ran about fifty yards and dropped, and he rode up and shot her again. He really didn't need to, but he wanted to make sure she didn't get up.

"Now that he had his first deer since being injured, he didn't know what to do with her. The doe was too heavy for him to load by himself, so he did what he always does: find a way to handle the situation. After driving the cart back home, he clambered into his truck. As luck would have it, when he placed the compound bow on the back seat of the truck, the bowstring snapped!

"Back at the field, Hutch trussed the deer up with one end of a rope, tied the other end to the pickup and gently dragged her home. Once there, he untied things and went to pick up a helper. The pair of them got her hung up, and Hutch did the dressing and skinning.

"The main thing about this whole episode is that Jeff didn't think it was such a big deal . . . and he still doesn't. It's kind of all in a day's work for him."

Two weeks later, when rifle season had at long last arrived, I went down for an opening-day hunt with the kid. Naturally, he put me on a stand overlooking Afghanistan, some nine thousand miles from the nearest deer. Meanwhile, back at the golf cart, he swiftly used his Browning to transport a large but completely uneducated seven-pointer to that great soybean field in the sky.

Yes, he generously allowed me to help drag, load, and undress the buck.

Now I'm not saying the kid is lucky, so don't get me wrong, but the third episode brought back memories of the Fountain herd. One warm, sunny November morning, Hutch decided to allow the penned-up golf cart out for a little exercise. He further reasoned that since it was an either-sex day, the Browning might enjoy a little recreation, too. Whirring through the trees, he caught sight of a likely dinner date prospect, got his cart stopped, cleared leather, and squeezed off.

He lost her in the recoil for a moment. But sweeping the scope back over the spot, he spotted the doe still standing there, probably wondering why the heck it was thundering on such a lovely, cloudless day. Hutch couldn't believe he had missed, but took no chances and shot again. This time, nothing was left standing. Motoring over, he was rather pleasantly surprised . . . not to mention shocked . . . to see two dead deer lying not five feet apart with no further worries. Oh, well, the more the merrier.

JEFF'S STORY REALLY IS AN EXTRAORDINARY ONE, AND PARTICULARLY CLOSE to my heart. I know of several other "confined" people who are just that. Many times when I think about Hutch, I'm reminded of a story my number one fishing buddy once told me as we were driving to a favorite lake. This gentleman, name of Ned Snellgrove, had ticker problems for years, and underwent open-heart surgery twice. He was discussing an acquaintance of his who had the same operation a week or so before his own.

"He always told me I'd better quit all this hunting and fishing and carrying on with you. Ever since his surgery, he's been sitting in his living room in front of a television set worrying about every beat of his heart and whether or not it will be his last. He says that consorting with you will be the death of me. While that's probably true, I don't think getting out and going hunting and fishing has anything to do with it. By the way, while we're going fishing this afternoon, they're burying that fellow."

Ned's gone on now, leaving a deep dark void in my life that surfaces with each and every fishing trip I take. Life, it's true, is what you make of it. Like the fellow Ned spoke of, Jeff Hutcheson could very well have given up, and few folks would have blamed him. But he didn't, and he never will.

Yessir, a man's got to know his limitations . . . and develop his capabilities.

24

DUCKS, HOGS, AND OTHER ORNERY CRITTERS

F orgive me, please. All of us hard-hearted hunters, a pox on us, are fully aware that the duck as we know it is on a single wing of extinction, flapping its way into nothing more than memory. And we hunters are greedy, uncaring clods who simply can't wait to see the last quacker or squealer blown out of the sky.

However . . .

Had you stood, as I did, in the midst of a bone-dry broomstraw field and watched at least a thousand woodies go whistling overhead . . . sometimes ten or twelve feet overhead . . . you, too, would probably have pulled a trigger. In fact, I pulled one many times, many more than I care to mention. Two ducks (finally) fell, and that, I had to remind myself, was it: "Stop! Quit! Don't shoot! Pick up your two ducks, go to your truck . . . while ignoring the hundreds upon hundreds of birds streaming by . . . and go grab a cup of coffee. For if you don't, there is a very good chance that your friend the game warden may materialize from the mist and tap you lightly upon the shoulder. And them there federal birds gets expensive."

It's a crying shame that the gullible, tremendously misinformed or simply downright stupid anti-hunters . . . you fill in the blanks . . . in this country refuse to admit to the fact that if it were not for duck hunters, their dire predictions may well have come true long ago.

But since we're into duck hunting and not anti-duck-hunting, it's also a shame that shooting in this broom straw field is so easily done. It's really too simple for a shooter, even one like me, to get his limit. Face it, if you can't hunt in ten-degree weather, with ice on the ground and in the air with every breath, sit in a leaking boat or quiver in equally-porous waders, what's the use in going? No pain, no gain, and all that rot.

As a brief aside, I will mention that Ol' Hutch helped a bit to toughen things up one very dry morning when the cooling rings on his golf cart axle overheated, melted, and fell off one by one as he motored through this sage field. Know what happens when red-hot metal drops into parched broom sage? I never smoked, stomped, and swatted so much in all my days, Hutcheson laughing his fool head off all the while. Humping it like a regular one-man volunteer fire department, I at least got it put out before the entire county burned.

And this episode put me in mind of another duck hunt, long ago but not very far away with my old buddy Jerry, whom you may remember from boyhood. That he ever made it to manhood is another book altogether, but Jerry knows how to go about duck hunting in the right and proper manner. Sometimes, however, he gets a little carried away, figuratively speaking. In other instances, he gets carried away in the literal sense. For example, check out the first duck-hunting expedition he and I were ever involved in. His account of what happened on this frosty morn will no doubt differ greatly from mine, but this is really the way it went down. Trust me . . .

FOR STARTERS, LET ME SAY THAT AS FAR AS WAKE-UP CALLS GO, THAT which we were about to receive compliments of Jerry was about as effective as a next-room cymbal player practicing at four in the morning. But to set the scene, we were to rendezvous with the remaining members of our roughneck ensemble at a home in the Altamaha River swamp area near Hazlehurst, Georgia. They were dedicated duck hunters all.

Yeah, to go wading chest-deep into a beaver pond, mercury hovering around the twenty-degree mark, with the ridiculous intent of ruining a duck's day takes a fair bit of dedication, I do believe it is safe to say. At any rate, Jerry was a novice duck hunter at the time. Evidence of this surfaced right off as I checked out his accessorized chest waders. In several places, strips of a familiar-looking, silver-gray tape were wound tightly around the rubbery material.

"What's the tape for, Jerry?"

"Ain't you never seen duck tape before?" came his outraged reply. "I hear this stuff is really supposed to bring 'em in, even without callin'."

None of us had the heart to explain the difference between duck tape and duct tape, or the pronunciation thereof. Besides, the lot of us was rolling around on the ground in merriment, unable to talk at all and barely wheezing out a breath every three minutes or so. That was Jerry for you: dumber and more gullible with each passing day.

Now I don't really know about ducts, er, ducks, but there was a trio of interesting wildlife specimens that something about Jerry attracted. This was a short while after our initial meeting and the comedy routine had closed. We had arrived at the iced-over water at swamp's edge some few minutes earlier.

Before we get into it, literally, there are some rather important factors that the uninitiated duck hunter should know about wading around in a Middle Georgia swamp, especially when the feat is being performed in total darkness.

First off, I was wearing chest waders and Jerry was wearing chest waders. Mine reach approximately three feet higher than

his do, because I'm now about three times his size . . . especially if waistline measurements are factored in. He's so short that he wears low-cut P. F. Flyers because high-tops would cover his bony kneecaps.

The significance of the measurements is that if I step off into a beaver run, there's much less chance that it will be the last you ever see of me than if Jerry steps off into one. Also, I carried a guide pole, which was nothing more than an old six-foot boat paddle with the wide end trimmed down for easier management when prodding the bottom. The pole is used for balance when slogging forward and for feeling ahead to make sure there are no sudden surprises in the form of sixty-foot-deep runs, which are nothing more than gorges excavated by deranged beavers.

Jerry, heh-heh, did not possess one of these poles.

"Better follow me, Hoss," I warned him as we started out. "If there's a spot I don't think you can make it across, I'll let you know."

It didn't take long, either, for the pole to find a hole with no apparent bottom. In appreciation for the good sense to bring that old paddle, I mumbled a quick "Thankee" skyward, then cautioned my pal to take a hard right and make for a nearby cypress. The tree in question featured a second, fallen cypress butted up against it. For the uninformed, root systems naturally have dirt built up around them under water, and they provide solid humps for under-sized hunters to perch on.

Now.

The aforementioned wake-up call arrived just as Jerry did the same at his waterlogged destination. It began from way off, growing in both noise and volume until it crescendoed off the trees like a sonic boom: "Yeeeeeeeeeiiiiiiii . . .!!!" or something fairly close to that. Folks in downtown Hazlehurst, which was probably in the process of being evacuated, likely thought the nearby nuclear plant was melting down.

Personally, I couldn't make much sense out of that first roar; my mind was focusing on how to walk, or run, on top of the water in waders. I didn't know what the heck was coming, but I did know it wasn't going to catch me if there was anything I could do to distance myself from it. I had finally pretty much gotten the hang of running on the surface and the waders were kicking up quite a good rooster tail when a second screech that I recognized as belonging to Jerry caught up with me. Just how it, or anything else, ever managed that feat is unfathomable.

"Coon attack . . . coon attack . . . glub . . . glub . . ." he squealed in a falsetto that would have been charming under most other circumstances. Looking back over my shoulder, but still not sure I wanted to slow down, I could see that he wasn't actually under attack, although he was nearly under the swamp's surface thanks to about a thousand gallons of water that had his waders pooched out like a hot air balloon.

The poor coons, on the other hand, also thought they were under attack, and were climbing like the very dickens to get away from whatever was making all that racket and slinging all that water. I turned back, waders now completely dry from the ankles up after blowing in the breeze, and fetched the victim of those nasty old coons from a foot or so under the swamp surface.

After he had been bailed out, to turn a phrase, and his pulse rate dropped below one thousand, Jerry jibbered out what had happened.

Seems that just as he reached the fallen log and got a grip on it, "it" sprouted fur and started to move under his hand. Remember, at the time it was as dark as a bear down a well, and Jerry didn't want nothing whatsoever to do with no furry crawling log in no dark.

When we pulled out later, many ducks in hand, there were coons swaying all over the area and popping valium by the truckload. We were asking Jerry various and sundry questions such as, "Were those mallard coons or wood coons you was a'huntin'?" and "Did the coons come in high, or were they just flying amongst the trees like those ducts that came in later?"

I wish I could fill you in on some of the replies, but we ain't managed to get a straight, or printable, answer out of the old boy yet.

We picked up quite a few woodies that morning, and there were probably others for miles around that died of shock and were never found. Serves them right for the episode that took at least a decade off all our lives.

BUT IF COONS AND DUCKS CAN BE CONSIDERED SOMEWHAT ORNERY, BE informed that they have a neighboring prime prospect for hot lead that can be downright bad news even on a good day. It is the wild, or feral, hog that haunts the same riverine swamps and palmetto bottoms as the ducks and coons.

In most areas, the hog is not even considered a game animal, and few restrictions apply to harvesting it year-round. But this can be as challenging a quarry as any you want to look down a barrel at. It can also turn intensely unpleasant when harried, and the big, bold, black Russian-strain boars will not hesitate to demonstrate that fact to you. They will also not hold back when it comes to using their ivory tusks to rip you from the South Pole to the equator . . . and any parts north that they can reach . . . given the slightest provocation and opportunity.

But on most occasions, the pig you've just come eyeball-to-eyeball with is going to turn tail and run like a very large and suddenly-scalded housecat, heading into the thickest cover this side of the KGB. I've mixed it up with both kinds. Believe me, the runner is infinitely preferable to the ripper. At least most of the time . . .

"THERE HE GOES . . . WHOA, TOO LATE . . . RIGHT, TO YOUR RIGHT, THREE of 'em; oh well, a tree stepped in the way . . . straight ahead, behind the palmettos . . ."

Behind the palmettos? If things started off sounding mighty like a dove shoot, well that's just the way it sometimes goes when hunting the wild hog. This was my first excursion after the bulky brute, and my fellow hunter was giving wild directions as a pack of porkers exploded from almost under our feet. Deer season was long gone, and billions of leaves were crunching underfoot like an overweight moose jogging on fresh pretzels.

In this case, the pigs had been rooting in a thick stand of palmettos. If you happen to be tromping through the swamps and find a spot that looks like a miniature Amazon jungle, rest assured that you are in prime pig habitat. As we came up on them, one of the three caught a glimpse of us before we could pick them solidly out of the undergrowth. Oh, we had been able to see parts of hogs and parts, as they say, may be parts, but you really want to pick your bullet placement on these targets.

Excitement of the chase aside, the object of the hunt is meat on the table. And believe me boys, what a Silvertip will do when it slams into ham is not really very appetizing. As I shouldered the rifle, the sharp-eyed hog's head popped up. In a flurry of squeals and flying mud, off went about a thousand pounds of stampeding bacon. Crosshairs settled on an opening ten feet or so wide that the pigs would pass through, and even though the first two beat me to the draw, the slowest of the bunch was presented with 165 grains of hello. He went down with a snout-full of mud, minus a couple pounds of pork chops.

As he fell, so did my heart. Right then, I knew I was going to love this kind of hunting.

The hunt, like the animal itself, can be wild and raw. That, along with the danger factor and the fact that hogs can be taken year 'round make it so very special. Most of the pigs roaming around free of charge are of the feral variety, which means simply that they were once domestic animals which escaped or were turned loose into the wild, after which they bred like rabbits on amphetamines.

Most hogs won't win many friends or influence many people even under the best of circumstances. But when they are left on their own, they tend to turn extremely shy and ill-mannered.

Tales of psychopathic porkers abound, and every hunter who takes to the hamhock trail for the first time expects to have to use everything from grenades to his trusty old survival knife to fend off razor-sharp tusks.

Maybe, maybe not.

The feral hog accounts for the bulk of the population, and goes all the way back to the Spanish explorers in the southern states. It is believed that the hogs on the coastal islands of the Atlantic are direct descendants of pigs brought over on Spanish ships. But the import of the European, or Russian, variety as it is more commonly known, has really added spice to jaunts in the swamp because this can be one nasty critter. The Russians are easily distinguishable, being bowling-ball black with an obvious mane down the spine. Larger in the front quarters than the domestic hog, they taper off to narrow hindquarters built especially for running down lead-footed hunters.

These Russians are really the glamor guys of the group, garnering publicity because of the alleged ease with which they slice and dice up dogs and hunters alike with no preference as to race, creed, or religion. Ever happen on a pure Russian-strain piglet and you'll think you're looking at a cross between a sow and an overzealous chipmunk, because there is distinct and quite characteristic striping on those chillun.

The hog is an extremely adaptable animal, eating just about anything it can get its snout into. Acorns, roots, and palmetto tubers are special favorites, with the menu winding its way down to deceased and decomposing partners in the swamp. Unlike deer, pigs are year-round breeders, with peaks in the cycle coming in the cold of February and late summer of July or August. Litters normally run from three to seven youngsters, with an average of five or six. Basically, as mentioned, they reproduce like house flies.

They also compete with deer, turkeys, or anything else possessing a sweet tooth for acorns, and believe they have gone to the proverbial hog heaven upon encountering a lonesome corn field. As table fare, most of the wild ones are quite good, but a big Russian is more sport than Spam. He tastes about like your granny's brogans and the meat has roughly the same texture. A young shoat, however, will make some of the best barbecue you'll ever flop a lip on.

Dog hunting is popular with a large fraternity of Southerners, but I prefer stalking or still-hunting. This consists of slipping through flood plains and soggy bottoms looking for both spoor and hogs. While you're at this, remember to make like a stump for several seconds each five or ten steps, and cock an ear. Many times the animals can be heard or seen before they know you're in the universe, a tidbit that comes in mighty handy with picking just the right spot to ease a bullet into.

Some, like the first slowpoke I popped, figure retreat is the better part of valor and waste no time hieing off toward Argentina when they believe they're in danger. On the other hand, some of those darker-colored ones don't appreciate intrusions into their dining rooms, especially when the intruders are accompanied by large-caliber companions. You may very well turn a boar's toes up with a .22 rifle or a shotgun slug, but I put infinitely more faith in a big-bore. From one of my latest excursions into the swamp, I believe you can see why.

"THAT'S ONE DAD-GUMMED BIG HOG," CAME MY OLD PODNER JOHNNY Fountain's urgent whisper. "Almost no way it's a sow, but I can't see teeth from this angle. Let's ease around this mudhole. Watch out for others on the way."

No need to worry on that account. The ground underfoot was as slick as a riverboat gambler's fingers, and we slipped and slid through swishing palmetto fronds all the while fearing a sprawl into the muck. Meanwhile, monstrous mosquitos were having a field day, even calling in their personal blood-mobiles from miles around to share in the harvest.

But we dared not make a sudden movement, and it was out of a fear that was more than spooking that huge hog.

Truthfully, within the overpowering solitude, funeral parlor quiet, and dank gloom of the river swamp, this was one rather spooky episode all the way around.

The big target seemed to be alone, but there was no way to be sure; surroundings were simply too thick. At any rate, it was moving slowly but steadily along, pausing every now and then to snap up some hors d'oeuvre or other. We were close, and I remember thinking that if this had been a deer he'd have whiffed us from a hundred footprints back.

My eyes were down among those prints, surveying a particularly nasty patch of mud. In the next instant, the rifle all but leapt out of my arms as Johnny, carrying a .243, yelled, "Shoot that big bleep; he's made us."

Not only had he seen us, but the boar . . . tusks suddenly becoming crystal clear . . . was loping over to clock our hundred-yard dash times. Or maybe it was our recently-tested blood types that interested him, because the gleam in those burning eyes didn't look any too friendly. Take my word for it gents: half-a-truckload of mobile, agile, and hostile ham bearing down on your belt buckle does wonders for production of adrenalin and other souped-up additives. There was no time to climb, even if the overhead hickory had come equipped with low-hanging limbs. I picked up his high-ballin' form in the see-through mounts . . . he was too close to even consider the scope . . . and squeezed off.

The boar didn't appreciate that much at all.

Although he stumbled and almost went down under the blow, he bounced like a ball bearing off a concrete floor, grunting a bellow like the locomotive he resembled in a couple other areas. The determination of an IRS agent and the fury of a jilted lover were in his eyes as he staggered toward my toenails. There was barely time to put the semi-auto's . . . thank goodness! . . . bead just above his snout and pop him again before he reached his destination: me.

This time, he went down like a lightning bolt had bounced off his noggin and lay there with a front leg waving above his rough, hairy, muddy hide. The old boy was four too-short steps from the gun barrel when he dropped for the last time.

Those several hundred pounds of pork wouldn't be much in the barbecue department, but that never crossed my reeling mind as Johnny flew down from what had become a very handy little pin oak and sidled over, still looking at the .243 as if it had been manufactured by Daisy. I shared his sentiment, lovingly caressing the old ought-six that had once again proved its worth.

About this time, quivering like an electric paint mixer from a terror that had never had time to properly introduce itself, I could have used a very stiff swig . . . say a quart . . . of Uncle Jack's Magic Elixir, direct from the distillery up north in Lynchburg; so could my equally shaken cohort, but those days were years behind us. Neither of us said a word. Instead, we traded glances that conveyed an identical message: this was one heck of a papa pig!

It seems that same thought comes to mind each time a big wild hog goes down hard. The old boys just don't seem to die submissively like their pen-raised brethren. They prefer instead to make it tough, interesting work, at times downright hairy for whoever's doing the ritual honors. And I don't look forward to any more episodes quite as spooky as this one.

Or do I?

25

CLOSE-RANGE HOGS DOWN ON THE COAST

The animal is one of the strangest-appearing I have ever studied, and I can't seem to figure out just what it is that doesn't look right. So, I simply sit, teeth chattering, eyes staring. Possibly it's my steady gaze that causes him to turn his head and stare right back into my face, making for an even eerier situation.

But then who knows? Maybe he's thinking the same thing about me.

Out of nowhere, the missing piece of the puzzle pops into place in my mind: it's his eyes. But by now, he's lost interest in staring me down with them and has turned back to more important things: like sniffing out a big boar. Dogs can be fickle creatures, but this one is decidedly not. He has a job to do, and he is very, very good at it.

It is thirty minutes after sunrise and thirty degrees as we ease the sixteen-foot jonboat around the salt marsh just below Savannah. I have been colder once, but that was three thousand miles north of here. And there were no hogs up there. Bears, yes; but no hogs.

From earlier proceedings, you may have come to the conclusion that I had learned better, but such was not and probably never will be the case. I am here to hunt hogs. Big ones. Mean, nasty ugly ones. From a boat. Well, partly from a boat.

The Ogeechee River meets the Atlantic Ocean hard by here, and along the coast are literally hundreds of miles of canals weaving in and out of the river and marsh of Savannah and Richmond Hill. These canals were dug well over a century ago to provide fresh water for tens of thousands of acres of rice fields on plantation properties. They average some fifteen feet across and are five to six feet deep at the morning tide upon which we were hunting.

The rice is long gone now, and sawgrass has replaced it. The grass tops are ten feet from the black, sucking mud that is the marsh's quagmire bottom, and woven together to provide some of the thickest cover imaginable. Sawgrass, by the way, is very aptly named; grab a stalk with your bare hand and you'll see why. You'll also very likely see blood flow should you try sliding that hand up or down.

A hunter has a hard day's work ahead trying to make his way through this mess, but for the thick-hided, wide-bodied, ivory-toothed boars of the coast, it's a parcel of paradise.

It is a different world, this hog hunting in the sawgrass. Back home, one hundred miles away, running up on portable pork is a common occurrence. It is one thing to be perched in a tree stand and hear a pack of pigs wandering in from a hundred yards away, then pick out a likely prospect for a 165-grain headache. It is quite another to have to fend off a razor-tusked boar at belt level from three feet in the muck of the marsh.

I had done the former many times, and while I didn't know it at the time, was about to take part in the latter. There are no tree stands here simply because there are no trees. Just water, mud, grass—and hogs.

The technique is to motor to the canals, then putt-putt through them as slowly and quietly as possible with the lead dog perched precariously on the boat's bow. This is the creature I was so closely studying. He is a fascinating mixture of Catahoula leopard hound and Alaskan malamute, with the Catahoula's trademark white eye and the brown one of a malamute. He also has a nose like you wouldn't believe, and uses it to sniff out any trace of hogs along the canal's windward bank.

Basically, the lead dog is in charge. There are two more dogs chained up in the boat bottom, to be used as catch dogs if needed. They are mixtures of some or other breed with a great nose on one side and a second whose basic nature is that of a rattlesnake with a migraine headache. They have three purposes in life: find it, catch it, hold it. Before long, we're going to discover whether or not they've missed their calling.

As we sidle along, the only sounds being the water lapping against the boat and my teeth chattering laps around my gums, I'm beginning to wonder again about this lead dog. He's stretched out seemingly as far as possible, as if yearning to catch a whiff of his quarry. But what happens if he does? And right then my question is answered.

The dog turns his head and stares directly at my partner, who's running the motor and also happens to be the one who provides him feed on a daily basis. Not a sound is made, but the motor is instantly cut off and the big dog hits the water. I cringe at the thought, but it doesn't seem to bother him a bit.

Now, there is near-total silence. The lead dog is a silent trailer, which means he will not make a sound until he is eyeball to eyeball with whatever it is he's attempting to run down. And finally, when he does open up, it's time to hit the bank and hie off through the mud and sawgrass as hard as we can go.

From hunting with dogs of all types for many more years than I care to tell you, there comes a sense of being able to discern just how serious an animal is when he's on a trail. What

I was hearing was half-hearted at best, and when I finally burst onto the scene it was easy to see why: the dog had run up on a sow and a half-dozen or so piglets. Maybe one of them would grow up to be what we were looking for, but for now we corralled the dog and headed back to the boat, thankfully quite a bit warmer after a half-hour of exertion.

We move on . . .

In and out of canals we slip until a pair of trails that are almost smoking-hot with hog sign appear on either side of the boat. This time, there's neither a look nor a wait for the motor to be cut. The dog bails out and hits the bank on the run, slipping through the grass seemingly with ease.

Our wait is not long.

The initial bark propels us into action, and then things really get intense. The next sound is not really a bark; more like a call for help. Another dog is frantically loosed to provide it, and he whips away, muscles rippling, right through the grass as if it were a golf course fairway. And we realize we've made a mistake.

The fight, for that is indeed what it is, happens to be going on across another canal and probably a half-mile or so further on. We have to get closer, and in a large hurry. The outboard's cord is yanked and my partner yells, "Hold on!" as we gun down the narrow waterway, small limbs from bushes and the ever-present sawgrass lashing at our faces. The boat speeds on, but the melee is moving. Twice we're forced to stop and listen carefully to pinpoint the location as the fight thrashes from island to island, across one canal and then the next, hog and dogs fighting and swimming to fight some more. Finally, the quarry makes its stand, and we beach a hundred yards away from a crashing of sawgrass, a roaring of dogs and the savage, deep-bass grunts and squeals of a furious boar.

I grab the gun and hit the bank on the run, my left leg immediately sinking above the top of a twelve-inch Maine Hunting Shoe into oozing black muck. It takes three desperate

jerks to free it and then I'm crashing along as fast as I can hurl my two-hundred-plus pounds, sawgrass be hanged!

Visibilty is measured in inches, not feet or yards, as the snapping of sawgrass blends with the fury of the fight. Although I can see and hear the grass going down as well as the tremendous squall of three blood foes locked in a life-or-death battle, I am within five feet of the boar before I can even make out what it is.

Were I brave enough, I could actually reach out with the rifle barrel and touch the largest boar I have ever seen on the hoof. He is, in a word, magnificent. In another, furious. And there is murder in his eyes.

I want to shoot him, but am so awestruck that I also want to simply admire him. I am being screamed at to shoot, but dogs feint in and out, and I can't take the chance. The yells, however, manage to draw attention to us, and since my partner is standing directly behind me, I suddenly become the boar's focus. I see the rage and realize with caveman instinct and simplicity that one of us is about to bleed. It's up to me to decide which it will be.

The report of the .30-06 roars across the marsh, but the huge hog stands and stares, his body shuddering. Then he moves.

There are no words to tell you how quickly he came, nor do I know how I even more quickly and precisely placed the second bullet. It entered the top of his head and came out the bottom of his jaw, grazing his concrete-block chest and putting him down instantly. He actually splashed mud on me as he fell and slid to rest with his snout between my boots, never to move again.

Came a silence in the marsh.

It was as if everything in Nature paused for a moment to pay tribute to one of its most formidable fallen warriors. Even the dogs were lying down, somehow realizing that it was over and if they had won, it was by the slightest of margins. They, too, were bloodied, ripped by the tusks that now are among my most prized possessions. There were stitches and weeks of recuperation ahead before the dogs would be returning to the canals. And while the blood I was shedding was from the sawgrass only, the outcome was mere inches away from being a lot different and far worse.

But then, that's the difference between killing and hunting.

26

THE OTHER HALF OF THE FUN

What happens, you might ask, to all that gory stuff hunters drag in from the woods and fields? Well, in my case, it is disposed of in as tasty a manner as possible. As evidenced by the fact that I haven't been able to peruse my toes from a standing position for some years now, I like to eat. Luckily, I also enjoy cooking, especially if it involves something I've invited in from the woods.

We're talking about a guy who can shoot, skin and gut a deer, then thin-slice the liver, slowly sizzle it in butter over a campfire, and gulp it down with the rest of the carcass hanging nearby all the while. But despite the fact that one couldn't exactly say I have a weak stomach, I'm pretty finicky about how things are cooked.

First off, it has to be thoroughly dead, as in spending a certain extra amount of time over the fire, oven, smoker, grill, or whatever happens to be handiest at the time. You have no doubt heard it said that, regardless of how you feel about venison, "If you ever try it like I cook it, you'll love it." I won't go that far, but if you don't like it the way some of my friends and I cook it, have yourself prepped for a taste bud transplant, because yours are shot.

We'll come up on some gastronomical delights apace, but there's always the matter of putting the cart before the horse. Dressing a game animal, or a domestic cow or hog for that matter, is critical to how that meat will taste once it's on the table. As my sidekick Travis Davis is fond of saying, "You just can't make good chicken salad out of chicken manure." In other words, if you don't have properly-prepared meat to work with, it ain't going to be fit to eat.

Take rabbits, for instance. Years and years ago, a fella presented me with the handiest little knife imaginable. It remains one of my most treasured trinkets, a super-light little jewel with a pair of blades as sharp as moonshine hitting the back of your throat. The first thing I do after tumbling a racing rabbit is take that knife and unzip the lately lamented Leporidae with it. Next up comes grabbing the hind legs that served him so well and giving the carcass a sling like popping a whip.

During this process, all manner of interesting things come whirling out, so a word of warning is in order here: hunting partners don't much appreciate being in the line of fire.

With a handful of bahira grass . . . I finally found a use for our local ever-present abominable stuff . . . the recently-emptied interior is swabbed out to cool. Few things in this world do more damage to the nostrils than a whole, deceased, and ever-growing rabbit hauled around in a hunting vest for several hours. Cooling that meat down takes a minute or so, and pays large dividends later. Ditto for a deer, even more so because there's so much more to stink.

And by the way, how do you dress a big buck? My hunting club buddies and I got into a verbal brawl a while back over a matter as infinitesimal as the starting point of undressing a deer.

It may be a small sidetrip from the recipes you're expecting to drool over, but I feel this point must be made. If you, too, have been wending your way through a deer-hunting career all the while trudging through the depths of ignorance about where to make that first cut, consider yourself enlightened: take the tail.

"Why?" you ask between guffaws, just as they did. Well, regardless of how fine a knife you're wearing, it's rather difficult to make steak of a rascal that's running seventy miles an hour and jumping thirty feet every other step. With that determination settled firmly into your gourd, ask yourself, "What's the best way to make sure a deer can't run after I've shot him?"

Many's the time a hunter has knocked a buck down only to see it pounce up and whitetail it into the next state. There have also been a few who led off with the old standby belly cut, or tried to make a steer out of the bull, then watch him go snorting off, leaving them with a dumb look on their faces and a useless knife in their hands. So don't ever assume that the buck has turned up his hooves permanently.

I know you're anxious to hear what you've been doing wrong all the years as you undressed things, so let me explain why the tail is all-important. Simply, a deer cannot take over three or four steps once you've de-tailed him. It's the balance factor, you understand, and that white tail is the focal point. You may have to call in an engineering expert to further expound on this matter, but I will attempt to explain the phenomenon in my own simple way.

Okay, fasten your seat belts.

The difference in a buck's equilibrium after he has been shot may be evaluated by computing the weight of a small piece of lead, which has just been inserted into one side of said buck. That weight ranges from, shall we say for educational purposes, lead from a .243 to lead from a .30-06. Since there's no balance-control computer in a buck's head . . . it's in the tail, and if you don't believe it cut one open and see . . . he can't figure out how to keep from running whop-sided. So, he falls.

Even if you're standing there with the tail in your hand and he looks as if he's escaping, don't fret. There's no way he'll make it far before taking a tumble. The deer doesn't know exactly why he can't leave you holding the bag, or tail in this case. All he knows is that he keeps bustin' his butt every time he tries to run off. At this point, he may meekly surrender, but it ain't likely. The required procedure in such a case is to re-equal his equilibrium with an identical piece of lead introduced to his other side. By this time, he'll be too tired from all that jumping up and falling down to run anyway, so the process can be completed with ease.

The next step is to clear out the body cavity, but unlike our rabbit friend, we don't snatch the buck up and sling him. Unless, of course, back surgery is on your Christmas wish list.

The body cavity is basically wasted space at any rate, and what's going to fall out is not all that important other than serving to clear out the hunter's olfactory system. Completing the gutting process makes the buck much lighter and increases his dancing ability greatly. Sadly, by the time the next rut rolls around, he will have lost his taste for the ladies who would greatly appreciate his flashy new do-si-dos.

Skinning is simple. Tie the subject's neck to an elephant or something equally substantial, then very carefully cut only the skin completely around that neck and just above all four kneecaps. Roll back the hide from the neck and insert a golf ball or similar-sized rock under it. Attach a chain to the ball, run the chain through a hide hole you've placed there for that purpose, then hook the other end of the chain to a truck bumper. Slowly drive the truck away from the elephant and— presto!—you now are the proud owner of a buck that can be busted for indecent exposure.

By the way, as you make that cut down the belly, use either a good guthook knife or your index finger as a guide and make a very shallow cut. If any meat at all is to be sliced, it should be your own. In that case, keep it mum as you sashay around the yard; the neighbors would surely tattle to the preacher if you happened to cuss.

If you are still not a true believer in the importance of tail removal, ask yourself how many tailless bucks you've spotted within those glorious autumn tree lines. Maybe you don't believe in the significance of my findings, but I have this de-tailed report to back my semi-scientific assertion. Besides, why do you think they call them whitetails?

I rest my case.

WITH ALL THOSE CIRCUITS, TRANSISTORS, ELECTRODES, WIRES, connections and such inside, the tail itself doesn't cook up so good—baked, boiled, or broasted. But the other parts, now, there's a different story. If you don't believe venison is among the finest of foods, go on to the second or third choice in this chapter. Me? I'll take a ham, please, and will likely wind up gnawing the gristle before quitting time.

As a human being who is at once busy as all get-out for about 11.9 months of the year but basically lazy as rip year-round, I prefer simple things. Like dressing a deer, for instance. Once the tail is off, a hunter can go the extra mile and have the animal sliced into chunks small enough to suit a mongoose, but that seems like an awful lot of extra work and, if you don't do it yourself, expense.

Your standard-issue deer doesn't come equipped with a whole lot of fancy accesories, and whacking off what few of them there are is a simple matter. If you really and truly don't know how to dress a deer, ask your neighbor; he knows everything.

When it comes to the cutting-up part, the everyday hunter can't go wrong using the quarter system. Flop your target on his back . . . after he has been skinned and gutted please . . . and heave down with all your bulk on the hind legs. Hear something pop on each side? That was either his hip bone breaking or your shoulder blade leaving for Pain City. In the case that it was his, flatten your knife blade against the side of the ribs and cut the ham off, then repeat for the other side. Yours? Don't worry; you'll make a great Quasimodo.

Repeat for the buck's shoulders and you have four large pieces of meat ready to be smoked, then baked. The ribs, also, are prime smoker and barbecue material, though a bit light in the meat department. Truth be told, when it comes to barbecue I can eat New York City sidewalk providing it has been dipped in the proper sauce.

The meat along the neck, as does any cut of roast, makes for some out-of-this-world groceries. But getting back to those hams and shoulders, it's time to go Cajun. The Acadian, or Cajun, people of south (the important part) Louisiana have a culture and heritage all their own, and a large part of that comes from the kitchen. I have an aptly-named Cajun Cooker smoker that takes charcoal, water, and just about any type of meat you care to throw in and processes same into the finest of main courses.

There are several different brands of these cookers, and all share the common characteristics of having a charcoal pan in the bottom, a water pan in the middle, and either one or two racks up top. Light the charcoal, fill the water pan, and when the coals are covered with ash, put the meat on the rack and forget it for several hours or even overnight. That's about all there is to smoking meat in these little jewels. As long as there's water in the pan, the meat won't burn, and will retain its natural juices.

Venison hams and shoulders are absolutely scrumptious prepared in this manner, but there's another trick or two that can improve even this flavor. Once the deer or pork or whatever has run the course of the coals, place it in a large roasting pan and drape it with at least a pound of sliced bacon. Dash in a teaspoon or quart of Kitchen Bouquet, according to taste, lightly sprinkle with garlic salt, and bake in a 350-degree oven for an hour. It will make its own sumptuous gravy and tenderize like you wouldn't believe.

This is an excellent main course for you and me, or twelve average eaters. If you really want to put all your eggs in one basket and be done with it, add potatos, onions, and a packet of onion soup mix before shifting the pan to the oven. Potatos usually take a little longer than an hour to get mushy, the way I like them, but bake them to your own satisfaction. You won't be sorry for throwing this other stuff in and going that extra mile.

A WHILE BACK, NEEDING SOME PHOTOS FOR A MAGAZINE ARTICLE ON pugilistic pigs, I called up an old friend of a friend, sort of the way it's most often done hereabouts. We trade trips for different species, depending upon whom happens to be harboring what at the time. When I mentioned wild hogs over the telephone, I could just see him shuffling his feet with dread. But, trooper that he is, the guy agreed to put me in the midst of a veritable posse of pork, for which I would gladly repay him with a next-daylight outing to roust some sleepy mallards. To make a long story a little shorter, he also introduced me to a superb venison recipe after we had been hoofin' it after hawgs all over the swamp. We were hot, tired, and aggravated, but I had my pictures when we placed our feet under the host's table to test-run the recipe. Later, kicking back in the truck, I decided that the four or so pounds of meat I had packed away before leaving were among the best that ever got past my gums. This is what you need, and what you need to do with it, to duplicate that feast:

One six-to-ten-pound venison roast

Three cups of red cooking wine (gets better as we go along)

Three teaspoons of Kitchen Bouquet (use it anytime and anywhere gravy might become an issue)

Salt and pepper to taste (very little salt and heavy on the black stuff)

One-half-cup of corn starch (the more the merrier when it comes to soppin' gravy)

Put the venison in a deep roasting pan, then mix wine, Kitchen Bouquet, salt, and pepper and pour it over the meat. Seal with aluminum foil and bake at 350 degrees for two-and-a-half hours, or until tender. Drain the wine mixture, thicken with corn starch, then return it to the roast. Proceed to the table and make every attempt not to eat too much. Trust me, they will all be in vain.

NOT SATISFIED? WANT TO GO HIGHER ON THE CULINARY SCALE? TRY cubed venison steak. It, too, is simple enough for you and me to prepare. Start yourself off with six to eight pounds of steak, because folks are gonna be hongry by the time it's served up. Sprinkle it down good with lemon pepper, then set it aside for fifteen minutes so good things can happen while you refill your glass. Rustle up a couple cups of buttermilk and a couple more of flour, then scrounge around until you've located enough shortening to flood an inch up from the bottom of a cast iron skillet.

Dip the steak in buttermilk, roll it in flour, and fry for two to three minutes a side in the hot grease. Simple, quick, delicious.

WILD HOGS HAVE A SPECIAL TASTE ADVANTAGE OVER THEIR DOMESTIC cousins because they work harder. They make me work harder, too, and I love them for it. But the extra effort they put out simply to survive means that they're made of muscle, not fat. In case you doubt this, push one too far, as I did, and watch him come after your backside. The speed of these things is unbelievable, and all the time they're bleeding they greatly desire to offer you the same opportunity.

Because they're much leaner, the quality of the meat tops that of their slob cousins. Then, too, when something has had ideas about chopping you into small pieces, dining on it is simply that much better.

When one of the local wild thangs has bitten the dust I love to fix up about twenty-five pork chops at a time on the grill, one of my favorite preparation sites for hog. If there happens to be any excess fat, I'll trim it off, grill 'em on very low heat for forty-five minutes, then—and only then—dip them in barbecue sauce. While most folks seem to favor sweet sauce for pork, usually a catsup-based variety, I lean to the other side, preferring a taste of lemon, mustard, and pepper. That's what makes cooking cooking, so suit yourself, but cut the chops an inch thick and prepare the way suggested. Don't think you'll go away hungry.

IF VENISON IS THE FINEST OF THE FOUR-FOOTED MEATS, DOVES HAVE TO be best when it comes to flying material. "Nahhh," you say, "those quail with all that white meat can't be beat." But I beg to differ. Tell you what you do. Go out and collect a big batch of each . . . I know, it's a dirty job . . . and compare. Birds need nothing more than salt, pepper, flour, and an electric frypan to become among the best of foods. Doves, gravy, and grits or rice, depending upon your palate, is about the best there is, but baking is one scrumptious alternative.

Pick up the packaged chicken gravy mix of your choice and dump it over a thumb-sized pat of butter and the birds in a baking dish. Drizzle a half-cup of water over the proceedings, then bake at 350 for an hour. If you think the quail are better than the doves, consult your local mechanic, because you have a screw loose somewhere. As a disclaimer of sorts, I will admit that neither of the dishes is exactly unpalatable.

There's one more very simple one that you might try. Salt and pepper doves . . . or ducks, which, especially in the case of woodies taste very similar . . . wrap in bacon, and bake at that magic 350 for fifty minutes.

Squirrel and rabbit, believe it or not, are among the items that have united these states since day one. The picture of the lithe, hawkeyed, buckskin-clad, brand-new American never failing to return from the woods without groaning under the weight of a three-hundred-pound buck is bull patooey. Rabbits, squirrels, birds of any sort . . . an occasional poodle or two . . . who knows what those folks chowed down on? I'd take bets that the first dynamic duo made up the mainstay of colonial diet, and it's still not bad fare.

You can put the two together in threes of each and work things out in even numbers. With three quartered rabbits and the same number of their rodent relatives, dig yourself up half a cup of vinegar and enough water to cover things in a big pot. Boil for twenty-five minutes and the meat will be ready to fall off the bones. Remove it, along with the water from the pot, de-bone, and set aside. Saute one diced medium onion and a half-cup of celery in a small piece of butter. All this takes about fifteen minutes. Replace the rabbit, squirrel and stock, cover with one can of cream of mushroom soup, add another package of that gravy mix, and then simmer for another twenty minutes. Believe me, it's not bad.

These are but a select few of the dinners and suppers that pushed me past more poundage than I care to mention. If you can use 'em, enjoy. I think you will.

27

PERMISSION GRANTED . . . MAYBE

T his is simply to thank a few people, and to relate an episode or two that I believe can make a great difference in the future of your hunting and mine.

Outdoor writers wouldn't be of much use to the world if they didn't have places to hunt, fish, camp, and tramp. Ever thought about it? Well I have, and often. We would probably run out of ink should I list all the gracious people who give me free rein to use rod, gun, and camera to terrorize the furred, finned, and feathered inhabitants of their domains. Therefore, I will gamble heavily and single out one, then pray the others realize that my gratitude for them also knows no bounds.

If you have ever pulled up stakes and moved to an area in which you know almost no one, you are aware of my situation when I came to my present abode some thirty years ago. There is always an uneasy settling-in period, and this reloca-tion was no different. Except that I had an ace in the hole: one Johnny David Fountain, whom you are by now well-acquainted with.

Having known Johnny for some time, I took part in his wedding as best man, a subject we still debate. This allowed me to meet and eventually become close to his in-laws. Believe me, boys, every man should be so lucky as to wed himself into this kind of family. His wife's parents, Kline and Seebie Scarborough, were the very symbols of southern grace and tradition.

Over these many years, Mister Kline has allowed me to euphorically ply my craft over the paradise of his holdings. Among my most closely-held memories are some dove shoots there. Mr. Scarborough is one of these folks who conducted "invitation" shoots. You got an invitation if you were extremely lucky. If you happened to be riding the dirt roads, heard us shooting, and decided to come ask the field master for a spot, most times you were welcome then, too. The gentle nature of the man hardly ever allowed him to say "no."

But if you abused that generosity, that's when Johny and I came in. We would gladly present you with an invitation of another sort, as in "If you care to shoot doves in this area again, please make it no closer to the fence line than Guadalajuara."

Well, at least it went something like that, and it still does.

The heat, gnats, sweat, gnats, long hours, gnats, and overall aggravation of opening-day dove shoots in the deep South can try the patience of the best of us. Most times, the birds just don't fly early. They are waiting . . . they've always been recognized as having higher IQs than hunters . . . for the cool of evening. But every third or fourth year we'd have a field so hot from first hour to last that a man could prepare Braised Beef Ribs and Ox Ragout simply by wrapping it in aluminum foil and taping it to a shotgun barrel. These were the good times, because they meant we'd have supper at Miz Seebie's table.

While Kline had been easing his pickup around the blistering field seeing to his guests' thirst, his lovely bride would be back at the ranch, whipping up such heavenly hash as hoecake biscuit and yup, you guessed it, grits. At day's end, we hunters would tromp in . . . after very, very carefully cleaning our boot bottoms . . . with cleaned birds by the hatful and, with a tip of the cap, dutifully turn them over to Miz Seebie. After she had ushered us out and into the most distant room that kitchen smells could possibly reach, she would proceed to transform them into the finest table fare this world has ever known.

Later, after the dining room door had been either unbarred from the inside or beaten down from without, we would find those birds swimming in gravy best described thusly: dip a thumb in it, wipe it upon your forehead, and your tongue will beat your brains out trying to get to it!

She did all this with a quiet grace and manner befitting the best the Old South ever had to offer. Miz Seebie Scarborough was as fine a lady as ever I met, and Mister Kline was her perfect match. She's watching the birds fly from above now, but never a dove shoot goes by that I don't call her up in memory. And Kline? He's still here, thank goodness, still special . . . and still receiving of my gratitude.

So are they all, those who have hosted us in the past. But it hasn't always been so simple.

Sportsmen make names for themselves, and so do those losers who cavort under the mantle of hunters and sportsmen. Take, for instance, an episode from a dove shoot in my early years.

A cousin from Daddy's side of the family . . . thus one I never saw much of coming up . . . had sought me out for a middle-season dove affair. He was aware that, even in my teens, I pretty-much knew where some birds would be flying. Cuz was told to come on down. He was not, however, instructed to bring along the two friends who eventually materialized.

"We'll go ask," I informed them after being introduced to the menagerie, "and that's all we can do. The landowner may find a spot for all of us or he may tell us to go where we can get a permanent tan."

As it turned out, we all had a place to bust a cap, and if we shot one time, the four of us shot four hundred. Along about middleways of the afternoon, we had already done that much damage. If not for the stupidity of Cuz and Crew, we might very well have put in a thousand or so more before the sun set. By the way, if one wonders why one would need a thousand shots to take a limit of twelve of these federal birds, one hasn't shot at them very often.

But getting back to our field, there was also a second set of federal birds close by that I was not, upon granny's gingham apron strings, aware of. Honest, fellas, I had no idea that there was a duck within a million miles, and at the tender age of sweet sixteen, had never even seen a duck in the wild. Well, and please excuse my squirming at the recollection, these weren't exactly wild, either.

The gent who had planted this field of runt-variety dove-drawing corn also owned a nearby combination juke joint, skating rink, swimming pool, and mineral-water health spa, complete with hot buttered popcorn and assorted other eats. Why his miraculous water allegedly could, on the one hand, make a kid grow to be king of the jungle and, on the other, couldn't grow kernels of corn bigger'n grains of rice always intrigued me. But the intrigue usually struck when the birds weren't flying; I didn't do much thinking during those times when they were.

And they certainly were humpin' it today. The afternoon was as hot as Anna Nicole Smith in a string bikini, so I decided to take a break and hoof it over to the shade of some big trees surrounding the landowner's nearby pond. It had been made perfectly clear to me over the years that it was slightly illegal to bang away at birds within a certain distance of a waterhole. The consequences of getting caught by the game warden didn't bug me nearly as much as what would happen when those who had initially made it so clear, Daddy and Granddaddy, got their large, gnarled hands on me. To that end, I had deposited my shotgun on my dove stool with

"Watch it!" instructions to Cuz before departing for cooler vistas.

To this day, I remain tremendously appreciative of that act.

Among his many other possessions, our host had a little wife who worked like a demon around the place. She was almost always to be seen behind the snack bar. As I discovered during my trek, one of the few great pleasures of her drudgery-filled life was hauling leftover popcorn to this pond and hand-feeding "her" ducks. I happened upon her doing just that, and she told me, in her quaint, quiet way, all about it. Little did I suspect at the time that there was another side to this gentle woman.

After my brief break, I was quick-stepping it back toward the oven that was the corn field when I noticed her heading back to that snack bar, mission completed. I did not notice one of the two miserable misfits who had recently become my unwelcome companions as he snuck up on those poor, unsus-pecting pond mallards.

BLAMBLAMBLAM!

From out of nowhere a twelve-gauge automatic almost caused me to irrigate the entire countryside. When my size twelves finally clomped back to earth, it was to a scene of flapping, levitating ducks, fluttering feathers, and a bat-brained moron reloading as fast as he could shuck shells. And then, here she came . . .

The five-gallon bucket was still in her hand as she ran like a greyhound and screeched like a tomcat with his tail in a trap: "Don't you shoot my ducks you bleepedy bleep bleep of a triple-bleep, and get your ugly double-bleep away from my pond."

That was for starters, and the speech went progressively downhill from there . . . especially after the ducks made the fatal mistake of flying over that field. Guess whose cousin they cruised over first? While you're at it, try to figure out how he connected on the first triple of his wing-shooting career. Could I have put my hands on him at that instant, said career would have been over.

I'm here to tell you boys, if you've never seen a full-growed woman racing wildly through a cut corn field and cussin' blisters on every shooter in it, you don't know what you've missed. She had the most impressive vocabulary I had ever encountered, even though my Uncle Clinton spent thirty years as a sailor and taught me 'most everything he knew.

When the shooting was all over and she had questioned the ancestry of everybody in sight as well as invoking all manner of plagues on them, their children, and their children's children, she got around to me. If you recall, I had been unarmed all this time, and she was well aware of it from our earlier encounter.

"This one didn't shoot no ducks, and you can invite him back," she informed her hat-in-hand spouse in a tone just now dropping below thunder. "But if I ever see any of the rest of 'em again, they'll never eat a bag of popcorn without wondering if it will be their last."

For some reason, I never received another invitation. Maybe it had something to do with a rumor that the guy sold off all his guns, hunting equipment, and farm land, retaining only the duck pond, before he retired to the asylum. And I never was much on popcorn anyway. I always kinda figured she'd remember me so as not to serve up one of the bags featuring hot butter and rat poison.

But you never can tell about demented folk.

ALL OF US SHOULD KEEP THAT SORT OF EPISODE IN MIND, BECAUSE IT'S A true story. Such goings-on tend not to get us return trips, as we have seen. On the other hand, I remember an old man who had, and still has, extensive holdings along a river near my home . . . holdings that hide some of the biggest whitetail bucks you will ever have an infarction over. Two taken off this place have made the Boone and Crockett listings, so I do not exaggerate. For years, there was never a hunter allowed here. I do not claim to be a miracle worker, but getting a single sidekick and myself in was nothing short of a truly major miracle.

And it all came about because of a venison ham.

I knew the old man vaguely from a couple of chance meetings, and he knew me from my writings. He was a long-time widower and very aware that I would almost surely commit any heinous act he could come up with for a chance at hunting those deer. Strangely enough, it was my cooking, not hunting or writing, prowess that had impressed him most.

"I ain't never eat a piece of deer that didn't taste like a boot sole, but I see you think you know how to fix it," he rather truculently informed me one night at a fish fry for some local politician or other. (So I didn't vote for him; the food was free!)

"Wellsir, I cook things to suit myself, but several folks have gained a pound or two eating my cooking," was the quiet and hopefully satisfactory reply.

"Bring me a piece sometime when you got a mite to spare, and if it's good, you can replace it off my place."

What did he say?

Replace it off his place? Did my ears suddenly resemble twin satellite receivers to be sure I was hearing right?

This is IT! Boy, if you've ever whipped up a piece of venison in your life, this 'un here's the one!

Remember the ham that is smoked, then covered with bacon and finished in the oven? I garnished one of those little darlings with every trick I ever learned in grandma's kitchen, then hand delivered it with steam still pouring out of the baking pan. When the old man's six-inch pocket knife blade almost fell through the meat on the first slice and he stared at me open-mouthed, I could already picture the crosshairs on one of those twenty-pointers.

For such a measly little guy, that was about the eatin'est old man I believe I ever came across. The potatoes and onions in the bottom of the pan had cooked down so tender that he could gum 'em without the aggravation of putting his teeth in, and the meat itself wasn't much tougher. He's never shot a whitetail in his life, but these days that old man's as excited about opening day as I am.

Oh yeah; the deal was that he gets one whole deer per season . . . ready to be gummed. It does not have to be cut into steaks or chops or ground into hamburger. He wants it quartered, smoked, and delivered a (large) piece at the time. He'll eat off one chunk for a week, so a buck provides roughly a month's rations. The problem is, the hams off those bucks are so large that they usually have to be cut into two pieces to fit into the smoker, so sometimes the feast lasts up to twice as long. But no, neither of us is complaining.

YOU KINDA GET THE PICTURE OF WHAT SHOWING YOUR GRATITUDE IN THE form of groceries can get you. But many times what is not left behind, as opposed to what is, can serve the same purpose. I refer, of course, to the common-sense approach of bringing out what is taken in, in the form of bottles, cans, paper, and other assorted litter. Trust me, nothing ticks a well-meaning landowner off more than to see his place trashed.

At a hunting camp early in my deer career, we had been finding empty brown bottles in groups of six and twelve and veritable Hefty bags full of other junk, along with a jumble of four-wheel-drive tracks among the pushed-down soybeans. Yes, this made us very happy, and continued for, as I recall, eight days. On the night of the eighth, our old caretaker . . . the same one whose reading session was interrupted by the buck bounding onto the roofing tin . . . used that old Mossberg pump gun to greet the truck with a twelve-gauge slug through its radiator and into the engine block shortly after a chained field gate had been pushed down, post and all. He thought he was about to be run down and touched off in self-defense.

From what our man told us, the two guys involved made a long and very rapid trip, afoot, back to the highway. Due to the miracles of modern technology which link truck tag numbers with computers, they also became closely acquainted with some of our local lawmen and their modest facilities. No, deer hunting at night while ripping up someone else's land is just not worth it, guys. And neither is leaving a trashy signature.

IF YOU HAVE PAID THE PURCHASE PRICE OF THIS PIECE OF LITERATURE and made it this far through its pages, I assume you are a member of the hunting fraternity, or at least not enrolled in the anti-hunting faction. I have absolutely no qualms about middle-of-the-liners who belong to neither. In truth, I have the utmost respect for the rights of the antis, even if that respect doesn't pertain to their methods. For instance, I have never harangued a blue-haired old woman, or man for that matter, for not getting up before daylight and hauling themselves into a tree stand in preparation for slaughtering Bambi.

On the other hand, I have had the same manner of folks present me with pure hell in a handbasket, and in front of a crowd no less. The best thing to do, I have at last decided, is to maintain a long-practiced, pasted-on grin while they are making complete idiots of themselves. It's not as much fun as teeing off on their teeth with a hoe handle, but neither is it as costly. It is not my intention to break anyone from eating domestic meat for the rest of their days, but unless you've ever slaughtered your own or have seen it done, please do not get into my face over the fact that I hunt.

For starters, I love the outdoors and just about all manner of the fair chase. Secondly, this is how I make my living, and I tend to get pretty nasty about threats to my family's security. But it can be a funny business, this arguing with fanatical animal lovers.

One old woman in particular has hovered over me like a dark cloud through the years. The fact that she doesn't know her butt from second base about the great love and respect I happen to have for animals is totally lost on her. In her eyes, I am a new-generation Hitler, sentencing any and all poor, defenseless members of the animal kingdom to a fate worse than Auschwitz.

"I wouldn't read one of your stupid outdoor stories again if I was being paid to!" she once vowed in a telephone conversation that probably turned the connecting lines a brilliant shade of blue. That was ten years or so ago, and hardly a month goes by that I don't hear something from her about my columns' contents. One of her particular favorites was Daddy doing a demolition job on that feist, a spur-of-the-moment accident that was instantly and for years after regretted by all parties involved.

Well, almost all parties, but then I never did like feists.

Maybe she has someone read my stuff aloud to her, but it's for sure and certain that she never misses a word of it. That provides me with no end of private and perhaps misguided pleasure. My top-seeded recollection of our verbal jousting came one after-church Sunday dinner at a local steak house. She popped up out of nowhere to scold me for some transgression or other. All of it was going in one ear and directly out the other, while I was busy sticking on The Grin. Nearby diners looked at her like the loony tune I have long taken her for, and when all was over, with not a word from me interjected into the conversation, she returned to her table.

A young lady, in her early twenties I'd guess, seated nearby motioned for me to come over. When I had, she uttered a couple of lines that I'll always treasure. "That old woman's been sitting back there eating on a steak as big as a Texan's hat!" she snorted. "I guess she thinks the cow they cut it off of tripped and fell to its death."

I, too, almost fell at the thought of that poor bovine, and at the guffaw of laughter that forced its way out of my straining-to-refrain jaws. Later, after I had cleared my eyes from the clouding mirth, the gal added, "You know, mister, it takes all kinds to make a world."

"Yes, ma'am, I guess it does."

28

WORKING WITH THINGS THAT BITE

Not only do we folks here in Middle Georgia hunt, we also fish. Sometimes, we even mix the two. If I've heard it said once, I've heard it a thousand times: "I'd love to have your job, hunting and fishing for a living."

Maybe you would. But it ain't necessarily so. Various editors over the years have seemed to come up with the same idea: if a story idea involved any critter with advanced tendencies to bite, I would be the writer. Whether or not their game plan was to get me completely et or maybe just gnawed on a mite, I'll never know. But there are times when I've wished I had taken up just about anything this side of convict duty to come up with three squares a day.

For example . . .

TWIN FORKS OF LIGHTNING RIPPED THE DARKNESS, AND THE SHATTERING clap of thunder that followed sent tremors through the dock underfoot. Rain pelted down like dried peas being poured onto an upturned washtub, adding to the storm's fury. But the minds of the four of us on that dock had neither time nor concern for the squall that was drenching the coast around Savannah.

For under that dock, in a veritable maelstrom of mayhem, one of the largest alligators ever seen in Georgia was going wild. The huge bull gator was doing everything within its awesome power to escape the clutches of a small wire snare and an even punier length of nylon rope that miraculously held it.

Naturally, with my luck, I happened to be on the other end of that rope.

Over the next couple of hours, that alligator . . . all twelve-feet, five inches and five hundred pounds of him . . . would be hauled in alive, trussed up in rope after rope, and hauled off not much the worse for wear. Up until this time, the only gator ever legally caught in Georgia that was larger was exactly a foot longer than this one, although not as heavy. For me, catching that twelve-footer was the experience of a lifetime.

With the re-emergence of the American alligator and its removal from the federal government's endangered species list, Georgia's Department of Natural Resources began a program of removal and disposal of nuisance gators. They had really become a problem, especially in the southern coastal counties around Savannah and Brunswick.

The breeding season of early spring is always the worst. When a bull gator gets ready to go mate-hunting, very few things stand in his way. Some of the major hindrances, however, are licensed agent trappers and DNR wildlife technicians. When a problem gator is reported to these guys, they go and get it. I had been told to tag along and watch, then tell the story. Simple, right?

So what's a problem gator? We'll get to that. And little did any of us realize what a story this one would be.

Society's encroachment on the alligator's domain, especially the development of coastal properties with golf courses and surrounding neighborhoods, is a major reason for man-gator standoffs. Golf courses mean ponds, and gators just love them.

In fact, one call about a nuisance reptile came from a course on Skidaway Island. It seems a six-foot bull gator had developed a taste for Titleists, although one golfer said he would gulp down a Pinnacle or Top Flite on the side now and then. This gator had become very belligerent about things when golfers took offense. Talk about water hazards . . .

But golf courses certainly have no monopoly on these bad boys. Just take a look at a handful of complaints received within a four-day span and you'll understand just how rambunctious these toothy critters can be:

> June 13: Savannah; five-footer in parking lot of downtown plant.
> June 14: Thunderbolt; gator in the middle of the road.
> June 16: Six-footer in the parking lot of another downtown plant.

When one of these situations arises, a DNR technician or ranger is contacted. He then gets in touch with a licensed agent trapper. They solve the problem by capturing the animal alive. Gators under four feet in length are relocated. Those over that are sold, either alive or for their hides and meat.

It is fairly unusual to be seriously injured by a gator during these escapades, but one wildlife tech I was working with came very close. A six-footer got a hold on his shoe, but he just got the side of it and thankfully not the foot inside. The guy had to take the shoe off, and the gator held onto it for two more hours. We finally had to take a tire iron to pry it out of his mouth!

Remember, these gators are caught by hand. While other state agencies across the South allow baited hooks or even shooting of nuisance alligators, Georgia requires the trapper to use either a snare or box trap and haul them in alive and for the most part unharmed.

The sets used to catch gators consist of a roughly fourteen-foot pole equipped with a wire snare and backed by a length of nylon rope. The trick is to locate the reptile, call it up by mimicking its "grunt" call, then loop the snare over its head. With that done, the pole is snatched back like a bass fisherman setting a worm hook with all his might. When the snare hits home, the fight is on.

As darkness descended on the day of the hunt, we had hog-tied four major problems. Two of them were relocated, the other two taken in for sale later.

The President Street boat ramp and public fishing dock in Savannah had been the site of reports of three gators. If you've ever been to Tybee Island, you've driven within two hundred yards of that dock. One of the gators was said to be a very large one which had destroyed five crab traps in two days. As fishermen on the dock above would begin hauling the trap up, the big'un would grab it and rip it away from its connecting lines to get at the bait and crabs within.

Usually when you see a big alligator come up, and he sees you, he'll disappear, and that will be it. But this one had obviously lost his fear of man. He was an accident waiting to happen. That gator was just too big to stay there.

THE CLOUDS SCUDDED IN AS WE WAITED FOR A CHANCE AT THIS GIANT BULL gator. Each of us knew it would be a close thing. We might see him, might not. We might even get a chance at putting a snare on him. But then, we might not. We would most definitely get rained on. We just hoped the lightning would stay away out over the water long enough. It was a long afternoon of waiting, wondering, and watching.

With an hour to go before total darkness, he surfaced two hundred feet from the beach. This was by far the largest conglomeration of alligator any of us had ever seen. One of my companions whispered, "I want that big son of a gun." So did I. But then he went back down.

The big bull would come up several more times closer and closer in, seemingly taunting us, always just out of reach of the snares. But with the blackness and the storm closing in, he made his mistake. A particluarly plaintive grunt was too much for the big bull to resist, and his massive head slid ever-so-slowly into the loop of the snare.

As it did, all the power that I possessed went into the slamming home of that snare. And I immediately discovered that there are few things in the universe more powerful than five hundred pounds of ticked-off alligator.

Despite the fact that I was being held down by a companion's grip on the back of my belt, the bull's first surge snatched my six-foot-two, 220-pound body six inches off the dock. My ribs slammed into the heavy wooden railing with a sickening crunch, breath "whooshing" out in a flash. Somehow, I came back to solid footing and heard someone bellowing to rear back on the snare again just to make sure. When I did, the bull responded by going into a wild, white-water roll across the surface.

It was lucky for us that he began that classic gator roll. All he managed to do was wrap several lengths of rope around his gigantic maw, effectively clamping it shut. Now all we had to do was use the rope to "walk" five hundred pounds of alligator down a sixty-foot dock, drag him onto the beach, then hog-tie him! This only took about three hours and every ounce of energy I could muster.

After he was beached, a braided steel noose attached to a stout aluminum pole was looped over the jaws. The gator was held down with the pole while two of us clambered aboard the bull's back. We wound tough strips of inner tubing around the mouth, all the while keeping a close eye on the gigantic, sweeping tail.

When the bull had at last been subdued, it required the four of us, as well as four more very interested onlookers, to carry him the 150 yards to the truck. I may make it sound brief and easy, but tremendously exciting and physically draining plus a little terror thrown in here and there are probably closer to the truth. All in all, there are maybe more tumultuous things to do than wrestle a five-hundred-pound alligator in a driving thunderstorm. But to tell you the truth, right off hand I can't think of any.

It's a little different than shooting at a whitetail deer. Make a mistake with a buck, and he'll run off into the next county. Do the same with a bull gator and he may very well follow suit . . . but with what's left of one of your legs in his jaws.

Oh, well. Guess I might as well admit to a certain, deep-down weakness when it comes to wild things that have the ability to bite back. They bring out the primordial in us that anti-hunters and such have long attempted to suppress. But we, as human beings, are hunters like it or not, admit it or not. To that end, and all things considered, I guess it seems right and proper that the hunted should have its chance, too, just like the hunter.

Speaking of which, let me introduce you at last to my greatest weakness of all in the hunting world. While we're at it, we'll ride down to the big hole in the ground and you'll meet one of the finest men I've ever known.

29

BEAR MAN OF THE OKEFENOKEE

T he swamp is, at last, quiet and still. Even the formerly welcome breeze has died to a whisper, taking with it the rustling and rattling of leaves and limbs. The hunter is thankful for that silence as he closes his eyes, takes a hollow, rasping breath, and channels all the powers of his senses into hearing only.

In front of him stretches a veritable wall of scrub pines and palmettos strangling in the grasp of a woven fabric of vines and briars. The area is part of that near-impenetrable morass known as the Okefenokee Swamp, and it is the closest thing to heaven for the secretive wildlife hidden within its borders. A member of that animal clan is what the man with the gun is listening for.

His hands tremble with excitement, anticipation, and more than a little apprehension as he maintains a death grip on the oily-smooth stock of the .30-06. The gun wafts the sharp odor of 3-in-1 oil, pleasant but seemingly out of place among the brittle-dry scent of the drought-seared swamp in South

Georgia's mild autumn. The familiar aromatic mixture goes wandering aimlessly through his mind as he stands stump-still, the hot, gleaming-white sand of a lonely logging road searing through thin boot bottoms. It's so peaceful that one could almost doze off standing up.

But suddenly the hunter's mind is jolted back to reality with what feels like two hundred volts of adrenalin-induced shock. There comes a yammering of dogs from deep within the scrub; then, minutes later, the sound of them turning . . . turning his way. Breath comes rasping shallower, chest tightening, entire being locked into the tableau before him. There's no doubt now: the battle is coming right at him.

With incredible speed and power, the bear rumbles through the thick tangle of the Okefenokee like a hairy fifty-five-gallon drum down a mountainside. It kicks up logs, bushes, and dust with equal ease while racing ahead of the lunging pack of dogs. Things are just too tangled to get a glimpse of it, but the man waiting by the trail knows it's there. And suddenly, just like in the hunter's dreams . . . or nightmares . . . the big black is in the open. It looks so much larger . . . and more menacing . . . than those behind the cold concrete walls of Atlanta's zoo, a couple hundred miles and a century or two of progress up the road.

The animal hauls up short like a dog on a chain as it realizes there's that sliver of road to cross and that its cover will momentarily vanish. The massive head swings to the right, and the burning slits of the bruin's eyes, red with rage, lock with those of the man, clearly sending a marrow-chilling message over the twenty yards that separate the two. For the hunter, as well as the bear, it's now or never . . .

BEAR HUNTING IN AND AROUND SOUTH GEORGIA'S OKEFENOKEE SWAMP has to be experienced to be believed.

This is not north woods country, with two-hundred-yard shots at animals browsing on dandelions like cows in a pasture. A fifty-yard shot is a very, very long one, and there are times when a hunter can literally reach out and touch his prey.

In fact, as you will see, this particular pastime can be about as hairy as the bear itself.

My introduction to the Okefenokee and its bears came compliments of one Jackie Carter, a living, walking . . . and that is a miracle in itself . . . legend among a close-knit bear-hunting fraternity that stretches all across the United States and even into Canada. Carter has trailed his favorite quarry through the northern states, into Ontario and beyond, but more of the Okefenokee than its Godzilla-sized mosquitos gets into one's blood. He is always drawn back to the place of his birth . . . the swamp . . . home.

Jackie Carter has seen the world, much more of it than he wanted to see if the truth be told, but the area around Folkston, Georgia, has always wooed him back. The story of the man is much more than one of a hunter. That he is still with us at all, much less able to trek the miles it sometimes takes to come up with a bear, is nothing short of miraculous.

Even in the early years, Jackie took to the Okefenokee with his father, Alton, and embarked upon a lifetime love affair with the place. It is extremely doubtful that there is anyone who knows the vast reaches of the wilderness area any better than these two. They have stalked, stomped, waded, and paddled untold thousands of miles through its heart, and are on intimate terms with its inhabitants. But it was the Okefenokee's bears that most impressed Jackie. Let's go back to the first one he ever saw taken, and you'll see why.

WHEN JACKIE HAD REACHED THE RIPE OLD AGE OF SIX, ALTON CARTER figured it was time for his son to take his first bear. Even thirty-plus years later, Jackie still shakes his head in awe as he tells the story.

"Daddy took me and two of my friends, one eight years old and the other one twelve, out into the swamp for me to kill a bear," Jackie related in his soft, slow drawl. "We found a yearling track to put in on, and Daddy figured that would be just about the right size for me, so we loosed the dogs. Right after they lit out on the track they started baying, so we figured they had the yearling treed. Daddy was going to let me shoot it out, and that would be that. But when we got in there, we found out that it wasn't treed. And it wasn't too little, either."

It most assuredly was not. In fact, the scene the foursome came upon was of a monstrous black, over seven feet and six hundred pounds of fury, battling a pack of dogs within a pall of swirling dust, leaves, bushes, and limbs.

"When we got there, the bear saw us, spooked, and broke right back by us. Daddy was totin' an unplugged shotgun loaded with number one buckshot and he shot the bear five times. It never broke stride, running right on through the swamp.

"That bear was tearing a trail that looked like a bulldozer had made it, the dogs right behind him. We didn't have any trouble following them, and the dogs stopped him again about a hundred yards away."

When the elder Carter and the boys closed in the second time, the bruin was lying at one end of a big cypress log, with the hunters at the other. The buckshot had done its duty. Or had it . . .

"He was just lying there like he was dead, and the dogs were ripping hair out of him and everything. But when we stepped up on that log, Daddy saw him blink an eye, and he hollered, 'Clear the trail.'"

The trail cleared in one large hurry.

"One boy lit out back down the way we came, the other straight out through the swamp, running like there wasn't even a swamp there. I didn't have sense enough to run and, besides, I wanted to see Daddy kill that bear. I skinned up one of two little bay trees close to the log. While I was doing that, the bear came after Daddy."

The pack of dogs consisted mainly of big, rangy, mixed breeds of hounds, typical of the type used all across the South for hunting bear and deer. But there was one, part collie and part airedale, that almost certainly saved Alton Carter's life in the next instant.

"The bear came like lightning, and there was no way Daddy could get away from him. But just before it got on him, that little dog sailed right into its face and slowed it down. Daddy had fallen to one knee, and he actually shot upwards at the bear, into its head and chest, five more times."

When the massive animal went down for the last time, it was three feet away from Alton Carter's bootlaces. But its awesome display of power and tenacity wasn't quite over.

"Daddy put in a killing shot, the eleventh time he had shot it. But before he did, that bear got its mouth around the little bay tree next to mine. When he shut down on it, that tree just toppled over. I thought I was twenty feet up my tree, but Daddy reached up and hauled me down. Both trees were four or five inches around, and you'd just never have thought a bear could do something like that. But that was a heap of bear."

When the hide was tanned and dried, it measured seven feet, two inches from nose to tail and was five feet around the middle. Yessir, that was a heap of bear."

SINCE THAT FIRST ONE, JACKIE HAS BEEN IN ON THE TAKING OF HUNDREDS of others all over North America. Through the early years and his teens, he rambled behind Alton and the dogs, hunting and frolicking in the Okefenokee at every opportunity. The love affair blossomed into one that would consume him, one which would last a lifetime.

But there came a time when he would be forced to leave his beloved Okefenokee, although he would be trading it for terrain that at times closely resembled the haunts of his boyhood. He was a man now, and this was a new swamp, one calling for men and men only. It lay halfway around the world and, like the South Georgia variety, came complete with its own everyday life-and-death dramas. But the story here ran much deeper than the hunting of bear or deer or any form of wildlife.

Here, man hunted, and killed . . . man.

The place? Vietnam. Where Jackie Carter's life would be changed forever. And very nearly lost.

"I WAS ONE OF THE FEW DRAFTEES THAT WENT INTO THE MARINE CORPS; just lucky I guess," Carter recalls. "I went in in October of 1969, and got the regular tour of all the scenic spots, like Parris Island and Camp Lejeune. They sent me to Okinawa, to the Phillipines, and to Japan. On the first of January, 1971, I went to Da Nang, South Vietnam.

"There were places around us that were kind of like back home, all of it swampy with rice paddies and such. In some spots you'd fall into boggy holes that didn't seem to have a bottom, and there are sure some of those in the Okefenokee."

The pain burning through his eyes is clear evidence of the battle still raging within Carter as he speaks of Vietnam. He was there only a short time, but it seemed like a lifetime too long. On Easter Sunday, 1971, he would get his ticket home . . . but at a terrible cost.

"We were at a place called Marble Mountain, and I was out with my group walking what was known as point shadow. I was the shadow for the man leading, and he evidently stumbled into a booby trap trip wire. I was walking behind him, and even though I didn't know it at the time, the Good Lord was walking with me.

"When the point man tripped that wire, a hand grenade went off six inches from my left ankle. There's no use trying to tell you what all it did to me, but there was shrapnel all through my leg, up to my ribs, arms, hands, chest, even in my back. In fact, there's still quite a bit of scrap metal in me now."

Carter would spend seven agonizing months in hospitals, suffering through operation after operation, therapy and more therapy, with doctors telling him all the while that the left leg needed to be amputated or at the very least that he would never again walk on it. But they didn't know the man very well.

"It was years before I was able to walk again like you need to when you're bear hunting, but I was determined to do it. Even now, well over thirty years later, when I go out and really test it the leg will swell up nearly twice the size it normally is. But I'm not going to sit around all the time and do nothing but worry about it."

Sound familiar?

His burning desire to get back to the hunt and to the Okefenokee had a profound effect on Jackie's recovery, and to this day he can walk the legs off most out-of-shape, would-be-bear-hunter-businessmen. Drawling, soft-spoken Jackie Carter may fool you at first glance, but you won't be deceived for long; the man is as tough as rawhide and can be as hard as tempered steel. He's also just as straight. But let's get back to his bear hunting . . .

VIETNAM WASN'T THE ONLY SPOT HE'S EVER HAD BULLETS FLYING HIS way, and, as he flatly states, "All the danger of bear hunting doesn't come from the bear.

"We were hunting in Canada once and had some folks from up north hunting with us. We got in on a big bear (which later weighed in at 438 pounds) in a corn field. He just ate the dogs alive, whipping up on a bunch of them the first time out, so we let them rest up a week before we put them back on him, again in that same corn field.

"The second time, one of our visitors was standing up on a hill near the field, and when the bear came out, it came by him. He shot and hit it in the leg, and the bear turned down a field road and came right at me. The guy never stopped shooting, and there were bullets from a high-powered rifle kicking up dirt all around me. I didn't know whether or not to run, and which way to run if I did, so I just froze until the bear finally saw me and turned off the road. I followed the dogs in and finished it off, but it was a close call. Believe me, I saw enough of that kind of action in Vietnam!"

If you think the story of Alton Carter and his six-hundred-pounder was a little too close for comfort, try this episode of Jackie's on for size. It shows quite a bit about the heart and fortitude of the man.

"We've had a lot of dogs, as good of dogs as you'd ever want to see, that have been killed by bears, and we've had some that have saved our hides. I remember one big sow bear in particular that I wounded and she ran around behind a tree. I followed her to finish her off, thinking she was hit hard, but when I stepped around the tree, she rose on her hind legs and came after me.

"I raised my rifle to shoot her in the head, but she was so close that she clamped down on the gun barrel with her teeth. I had to take it away from her to shoot her again, and if it hadn't been for six dogs jumping in and pulling her down, I never would have been able to do it. As it was, I just reached out and put the barrel on her neck to end it."

Such were the stories I had heard before being invited to tag along with Jackie on one of his Okefenokee forays. My chance finally came with the final weekend of South Georgia's three two-day hunts. A hunter may kill one bear per year and only has six days in which to do it. Jackie's skill and diehard attitude help even the odds quite a bit, but it's still pretty dicey on getting a shot. On those six days, the Carter crowd managed to take a dozen bears. I will never forget my first trip . . . or the way it ended with that bear barreling through the scrub . . .

WE FOUR-BY-FOURED INTO THE MIST-SHROUDED OKEFENOKEE AS THE gray of first light was waking the world. The tract we would be hunting was criss-crossed by narrow, man-made dirt roads locally called tracks. Just before dark on the evening before a hunt, leafy limbs would be cut and tied to truck bumpers, then dragged up and down these roads, wiping them clean.

Next morning, Jackie and other veteran hunters would ride these tracks looking for another type of track—bear—crossing them. If it was large enough or fresh enough, the dogs would be loosed from their pickup boxes and turned in to hunt.

All the trucks were linked by CB radio, and when a proper spot was located, we were called together. That's when the "safety meeting" began, with Jackie doing the honors as head spokesman.

"We're going to put the dogs in right here," he said with a sweeping point, "and the bear will head this way. Just across that pasture is the federal part of the Okefenokee, where we can't go. That's where he wants to go. We'll put y'all on stands along the track (road). Everybody stay on the same side of the track, wait for the bear to cross, then shoot across the track. Don't shoot in front of you and don't shoot to the side of you, because there will be dogs and handlers out front and other hunters on each side. You sure don't want to shoot one of your friends with a high-powered rifle, and some of these dogs cost up to four thousand dollars. If you shoot him, you've bought him."

Carter knows a thing or two about getting a point across.

We spread out and wait. The dogs are freed, and immediately set up the call. But when they have done their best and appear thorn-torn and bloody along the dirt track some thirty minutes or so later, we discover that the bear has won. It was a big one, its oval, deep-padded print measuring six inches across.

Ironically, while we were shivering in the dawn chill during the safety meeting, with the dogs yowling from their boxes, the bear heard everything and decided to make an early exit for the protection of the swamp. That's how big bears get to be that way.

An hour later, the CB crackles with instructions to a different bear track, and we're off. This trail takes us into a two-hundred-acre terror of scrub, with visibility near zero. Hunters are put out to surround it, and the dogs are freed. Within minutes, we get the word: as many as three bears running in circles inside.

From the edge of the track I'm perched on, I pace inward in curiosity, just to see what the distance into the no-see-through stuff is. I take five steps, look left and right for a lane that's not there, and decide to go back to the track. That's how thick it is, and that's why dogs are used. A bear could run forever, undetected, in this mess.

But shortly, the spang-spang of a .30-30 lever action comes rolling from the other side of the brush. The CB word is a single one: missed.

Thirty more minutes hobble arthritically by before two more shots are heard. Different hunter, same result. Finally, after an hour of standing wired for action in the now-boiling sun, another pair of shots booms out. This time, there was enough of an opening to get in perfect bullet placement, and it was over.

Why the second shot? Back to the safety meeting.

"When you shoot a bear and he goes down, go up to him and shoot him again at the base of the neck," Jackie is saying. "I don't care how dead he is, put the gun barrel on him and pull the trigger. 'Dead' bears get up and run off, and sometimes they come after you. And the most dangerous time of all for a dog is when the bear is down and hurt, but not dead. The dogs can catch him then and that's not always the best thing for the dogs."

Later I would notice what were obviously streaks of blood running from the front to the back of a six-foot bed of a fellow hunter's truck. Turned out that one of the dogs had gotten to that first bear, or the other way around, before the final shot could be administered. The dog's muzzle had been bitten completely through. It was painful, but would heal. Blood had streamed down the side of the truck as the hound held its head out of the dog box.

As the sun continued to rise and the heat grew worse, dogs as well as hunters began to suffer. Dogs need moisture in the bear tracks to be able to trail them, and things were drying out mighty fast. But there was that one last chance, and I was more than willing to take it.

WHEN THE BEAR BURST THROUGH THE BUSHES BEFORE HALTING BY THE track, he had rumbled right over where I went in to check on avenues for shooting. Now, as I swung the ought-six, both of us had decisions to make.

Less than a hundred yards away in the bear's direction lay the pickup truck and CB that had kept us abreast of what was happening. To the left was another hunter, roughly the same distance away, but no factor in whether or not to shoot. There were no dogs around yet, so that wasn't a problem either. What would the bear do? He could charge, turn tail and head back the way he came, or cross the track.

All this went fleeting through my mind in mere milliseconds as I distilled years of handling guns and the terrific excitement of a front-porch bear into the decision of whether or not to shoot. We glared at each other, burning, malevolent eyes to four-power optics, before he made the first move.

As the bear, still facing me, bunched bulging muscles to go bounding one direction or the other . . . and I'll never know . . . the Silvertip punched him directly between the eyebrows.

There was no snarl at the whiplash of the bullet; no final charge that had to be turned; no worry about snatching dogs out of danger. There was nothing but a very suddenly very dead bear and a couple million butterflies flapping wildly inside me amid a tremendous sense of triumph as I let out my loudest and best Rebel yell.

And, oh yeah . . . there was also one final neck shot.

Jackie Carter

David Frost

Jeff Hutcheson

Elliot Harrison

J. T. Turner

About the Author

DARYL GAY is an award-winning outdoors writer who lives in Dublin, Georgia, but is most at home slipping silently inside the treeline, rifle or shotgun in hand. He is an avid fisherman, but the consuming passion of the hunt and the hunters he's met along the way have provided the driving forces in his life.

Daryl's stories have appeared in newspapers and magazines across the South, and he has been a columnist for *Georgia Outdoor News* magazine for fifteen years.

Wife Cheryl and sons Coby, Dylan, and Myles are also welcome to tag along afield on any occasion—as long as they're quiet.